I0449834

Wee Tim'rous Beasties

by Douglas English

TO MY DEAR CHILDREN BRYAN AND WINNIE

PREFACE

For permission to include in this volume "The Awakening of the Dormouse," "The Purple Emperor," "The Harvest Mouse," and "The Trivial Fortunes of Molge," I have to thank the Editor of the Girl's Realm, and for "The Story of a Field Vole," and "The Passing of the Black Rat," I am indebted to the courtesy of the Editor of Pearson's Magazine.

DOUGLAS ENGLISH.

HAWLEY, DARTFORD, September, 1903.

CONTENTS

"WEE TIM'ROUS BEASTIES"

MUS RIDICULUS

Mus ridiculus! The taunt had been flung at him by a stout field-vole, and, by reason of its novelty as well as of its intrinsic impertinence, had sunk deep into his memory. He had felt at the time that "Wee sleekit, cowrin', tim'rous beastie" was but a poor rejoinder. But he knew no Latin and chose what was next in obscurity. Besides, he was a young mouse then, and breathless with excitement.

The scene rose vividly before him--the moon shining grimly overhead, and the mouse-folk stealing from the half-threshed stack across two fields into the farmstead.

Since that night he had never entered a wheat-stack, for fear of the leaving of it. For there are some things which, from a mouse standpoint, will not bear repetition.

There had been a grey, slanting ghost-swish above, and his brother had vanished skywards from within an inch of his side. He had turned to stone before two ice-cold eyes, and realized the honest yard of snake behind them. A stoat had passed him with its mouth too full to snap--and all within two fields.

Mus ridiculus! The vole was not so far wrong after all, for could anything, whose intelligence was otherwise than laughable, be in his present plight? In front of him were three horizontal wires, above him were nine more, on either side an upright wooden wall, behind him a slanting one, whose lower extremity nipped his tail. On the floor lay innumerable crumbs of evil-smelling cheese.

When the door of the trap had clicked behind him, he had naturally been startled. His fright, however, was due not so much to his surroundings--he was used to close quarters--as to the forcible restriction of his tail. Still, the cheese was within easy reach, and he had determined to enjoy it. Indeed, he ate his full. Now, cheese on an empty mouse stomach acts as an intoxicant. He had fallen into a drowsy slumber, crouched in a back corner of the trap, and so he slept for an hour.

His awakening was gradual, but rude. It was due to a steadily increasing discomfort in his tail. It was not the first time, however, that he had realized that a long, tapering tail has its disadvantages as well as its uses. As a controllable balancing-pole, there is probably nothing to equal it. As a parachute, it serves its purpose in a precipitate leap. As a decoy, it frequently disturbs the enemy's aim. But, when once it is firmly jammed, it is liable to congestion, and this is what awoke the mouse.

At first he was inclined to treat the matter lightly. He had been caught by the tail often enough, after all. He tried the normal methods of release. Swinging round on his haunches, he caught the offending member between his two fore-paws, so as to ease it out by gentle side-shifts. Then he brought his tongue into play as a lubricant. Then he simply pulled. By this time he was fairly awake and could feel.

It was unfortunate that a door banged above him, for, mouse-like, he leapt forward with all his leaping strength. The leap freed him, but at a price, and the price was his tail, or, rather, all that made a tail worth having. For the first half-inch it proceeded soundly enough, a series of neat, over-lapping, down-covered scale-rings, then, for the next two-and-three-quarter inches it presented all the naked hideousness of an X-ray photograph. It was not so much the pain he minded as the indignity, and he surveyed himself with gloomy disgust. There was, however, just a grain of consolation. With an imprisoned tail, escape was impossible. Now that he was free to move, there was surely a chance of squeezing through those bars. He must take heart and gird himself for the struggle. No mouse, however, if he can help it, enters upon a serious undertaking ungroomed. So he sat back on his hind legs and commenced an elaborate toilet. First he licked his tiny hands and worked them like lightning across and down his face. This he continued for a full minute, until his whiskers bristled like tiny needles, without a speck of dust throughout their length. Then he combed the matted fur of his waistcoat with his teeth, and smoothed and polished it until every hair was a gleaming strand of silk. Finally he turned his attention to his back and sides, twisting his body cat-fashion to reach the remoter portions of himself.

Once, in the middle of his operations, he stopped with a jerk and sat up motionless, save for a tremulous quiver of his muzzle. There was certainly something moving close at hand. Long before the faint vibration had reached his ears, his whiskers had caught it and flashed their danger-signal to his brain. It was only a cockroach, however. As it came in sight, he snapped at it viciously through the bars, and squeaked at its precipitate flight. Not that he grudged it the cheese crumbs, but his nerves were on edge, and it had frightened him.

Body, head, and feet alike, were sleek and resplendent before he caught a glimpse of his disreputable tail. He was dubious as to whether polishing would have any beneficial effect on its appearance; but the stump, at any rate, must be healed, and to do this he set to work with nature's remedy. Taking the stripped portion in his fore-paws--for, to his astonishment, he found that he could not move it otherwise--he pulled it gently between his hind legs up to his mouth. It parted like a pack-thread. Somehow he felt indifferent. A rigid, lifeless tail was little use, after all. He was bound to lose it sooner or later, and he was too old to care what the other mice might think. Besides, as the father of a hundred and fifty, he was surely entitled to set the fashion. He licked the stump until it felt easy, shook himself once or twice, gave his whiskers a final polish, and prepared to walk out.

He felt sleek enough to squeeze through anything--confident, too, though just a trifle thirsty. It must have been the cheese, for the hot taste still lingered in his mouth, and he loathed the sight of the remaining fragments. He flicked them into a corner and carefully surveyed his position. The bars stretched at even intervals, above and in front. He tried each one separately and found that, with one exception, they were fixed and immovable. The exception was number three from the front above him. It was easily distinguishable from the others, for a curved wire swung free from its centre. When he gripped his fore-paws round it, he felt it twist in its sockets. Why did that curved wire rattle about when he touched it? Those from which he had stolen so many dainty morsels in the past had seemed fixtures. Perhaps he had gone too recklessly to work this time. He had certainly been extremely hungry. Anyhow, the bar from which it hung was loose--he would work that clear of the wood in no time, and so gain freedom.

He raised himself on his hind legs and commenced gnawing vigorously at the socket-hole. The position was a terribly strained one, and time after time his teeth slipped and met with a scrunching jar upon the metal.

Then he leaped up and swung head downwards, gripping the bars with all four feet. In this position he could at least nip the cross-piece, and worry it with his teeth. Every muscle of his small body was strained to the utmost. The bar rattled in its sockets, slipped round once or twice, bent the merest trifle, and--jammed immovable as the others. He felt that he was wasting his strength, and dropped sullenly to the floor. He had never been so thirsty in his life; yet, true to his instincts, he started to wash his face and smooth his draggled fur afresh.

This time it was a harder task, for his mouth was parched and tender, and his fingers ached with exertion. Still, he managed to put his whiskers into proper trim, and pulled himself together, with every sense alert for the air-current which should betray some outlet.

He explored every cranny of his prison, slowly and calmly at first, then with increasing anxiety and speed. By using all his strength, he raised the door a tail's-breadth. For fully an hour he struggled at this chance of exit. Five times he forced his nose under the sharp wood edge, and sobbed as it snapped back, mocking at his failing strength.

It was not until he was sick with weariness, and mad with thirst, that he lost his head. Then he flung himself recklessly in every direction, bruising his poor body against the unyielding bars, desperate, grimy, pitiable.

Nature intervened at length, and lulled him into a semi-conscious, dream-bound indifference.

* * * * *

There was something to be said for the stack-life, after all. All good stacks come to an end, but, while they last, it is honey for the mouse-folk. Picture to yourself the basement of a wheat-stack, occupied by a flourishing mouse colony--five hundred tiny souls, super-abundance of food, and no thought for the morrow. The companions of his youth stole into his dream with all the vividness of early impressions. The long-tailed wood-mouse--a handsome fellow this, with great black liquid eyes, and weasel colouring; the harvest-mouse, that Liliputian rustic to whose deft fingers all good mouse-nests are indiscriminately assigned; the freaks, white, black, and nondescript; and, finally, the great brown rats.

In the presence of the latter he had always felt nervous, but he had recognized their usefulness. Had he not seen four of them combine and rout a weasel? In the midst of plenty they were harmless enough, at least they had never molested him. Moreover, they were the main tunnel builders, and it was refreshing for a mouse, who had wormed his way through two yards of powdery corn-husks, to find a run where he could stretch his limbs and scamper.

And what wild scampers those were! For free, unimpeded, safe racing, there is nothing to touch the rat tunnels of a wheat-stack.

He was a fortnight old when he first ventured out into the unknown. He remembered but little of his earliest sensations, only the vague comfort of nestling with six companions under his mother's soft fur, and the vague discomfort caused by her occasional absence. But that first journey was unforgetable. The maze of winding burrows, the myriad eyes peering at him through the darkness, the ceaseless patter of tiny feet, before, behind, and on all sides, the great brown rat sniffing dubiously as it passed, the jostling, the chattering, the squeaking. He had been a proud mouse when he had returned, and told his faint-hearted brothers what the great world outside was really like.

* * * * *

It was a bluebottle that roused him. It floundered heavily against the bars, crawled through, and brushed across his nose. No! he was not dead yet, but the bluebottle soon would be. He leaped at it, and, to his amazement, fell short and missed. Yesterday, he had cleared a flight of stairs with one light-hearted bound, and left a bewildered kitten at the top. He sank back heart-broken, and the bluebottle circled solemnly overhead, buzzing, buzzing, buzzing.

* * * * *

Buz-z-z-z! whir-r-r! He was back in the wheat-stack once more, listening to the dull humming of ten thousand bluebottles. From without came the sound of heavy tramping feet, whirring wheels, rough, human voices. The wheaten mass rocked and vibrated above his head: half the runs were choked, and he, with twenty more of his kind, sat cowering in a corner of the foundations. Nearer and nearer came the voices, for the thrashing had commenced at sunrise, and now, as evening approached, three-parts of the stack were gone. Only once had he ventured to the edge of his shelter and looked out. A pair of grinning jaws crashed against the outlet, and snapped within a hair's-breadth of his nose. It was his first sight of a terrier, and he realized that to break cover was certain death.

Death, indeed, was very busy outside. Every minute a dog's yelp, the shout of its master, and the dull thud of a bludgeon, told plainly enough the tale of some unhappy rodent's dash for freedom.

And so the sun went down blood-red.

It was midnight, however, before the remnant gathered themselves together, and agreed on flight. The trek was headed by an old brown rat. Of the dozen that survived it, he was the only mouse.

* * * * *

Better, after all, to have never finished the journey, and, yet, why should he complain? He had lived longer than most, and had had his supreme moments.

* * * * *

"'The mouse behind the mouldering wainscot shriek'd.'"

He had been dozing behind the wainscot in the dining-room, and the squeak of irritation had been due to a passing spider. The apt quotation reached him through the panel.

"Squeaked, surely?" The correction came in a soft, woman's voice.

"No, shrieked; I am certain of it."

"Squeaked, I think; a mouse doesn't shriek."

"Ah, but this mouse had a poetic licence."

"Look it up."

"I will."

The book was taken from within two inches of where he sat.

"'Shrieked' it is."

It amused him vastly, for he had never shrieked in his life.

"Do you like mice?" It was the first voice speaking again.

"Hate them--smelly little things."

"Do you remember that thing of Suckling's?--

"'Her feet beneath her petticoat, Like little mice, ran in and out, As if they feared the light.'

"Pretty, rather, I think."

"What's pretty?"

"Oh, I don't know--your feet, I suppose."

He felt disappointed. Surely it was the feet that profited by the comparison. Still, he knew that the whole conversation would amuse his wife, and rushed off to tell her before he should forget it.

He had been rather anxious about her of late. Only the previous evening he had peeped from behind the bookcase and seen her backed into a corner, and defying six feet of solid humanity with brandished paws. Behaviour of this kind was courageous, but unmouselike, and would assuredly get her into difficulties.

He found her in the midst of tiny wisps of paper, thread, and wool, that had been her chief concern for three days past.

"Did you ever shriek?" he cried.

"No," she replied; "but I shall do if you can't be less clumsy."

He looked at her in amazement. Then the truth burst upon him. He was the father of seven, and was awkwardly seated upon three of them.

* * * * *

She had been a good wife to him, this first. He had three especial favourites, the first, the third, and the sixth, but it was unquestionably the first that he had been the most proud of. She was a veritable queen among mice, and he had fought five suitors to win her. The madness of it! He had gone from basement to ceiling, challenging all and sundry who ventured to dispute his claim. But she was worth it. All he knew of house-life he had learnt from her. It was she who showed him the way to rob a trap. First she would sit upon the spring-door and satisfy herself that it was not lightly set, then with flattened body she would steal beneath it, and push, instead of pull, the bait.

Under her guidance he learnt every nook and corner of the rambling house, the swiftest ways from garret to cellar, the entrances and exits of the runs, their sudden drops and windings, and all the thousand intricacies of architecture that make life under one roof possible for both mice and men.

He learnt, moreover, from her that fighting the cat was merely a game of patience, and that even the human male has a warm corner in his heart for the mouse that is bold enough to approach him.

And yet she fell a victim to the cat herself. It was out of pure bravado that she crossed its tail to prove that a cat with its eye on a mouse-hole has no eye for anything else.

He, too, had been in the cat's clutches once. It was hardly to his discredit. He had been with his wife at the time, had heard the sneaking footfall, and was in the act of pushing her into shelter when he felt himself pinned down.

The moment the cat's paw touched him he had relaxed every muscle and feigned death. The ruse succeeded. The cat loosened her hold, and he had a two-yard run before he was pinned afresh.

Then he was flung into the air and caught like a ball, dashed aside and caught again, and swung, and twirled, and shaken, until he was too dazed to move a limb, and lay, a yard away from his tormentor, staring stupidly into her eyes. Yet he had received no mortal hurt.

He owed his rescue to a human hand, and the hand smoothed his poor draggled coat, and pushed him inside his hole, while the cat complacently purred. For two long hours he lay just within the entrance, exhausted, but unattainable, and for two long hours the cat sat waiting for his reappearance. Whenever he raised his head their eyes met.

* * * * *

Their eyes were meeting now. Consciousness returned to him for a few seconds, and in those few seconds his blood turned to water, even as before. She sat on the window-ledge outside. Her muzzle was pressed against the glass, and he could trace the snarling curl of the lips, which just revealed her teeth. He cowered back as far as possible. Sooner or later she would find her way inside--and then?

* * * * *

He had only once been actually caught, but he was very near it in the corn-bin. Now, a house-mouse has no right whatever in the corn-bin, and yet it was a point of honour with the house-mice that they should visit their stable relations at least once a week. It was the love of excitement, more than the love of corn, which impelled them.

Crossing the yard was always risky work, whether one skirted the shadowy side of the wall, or made a bold dash in the open. Then the simplest way into the storeroom was through a hole in the corner of the window-sill, and to reach this meant a clamber along a half-inch ledge, with the certainty of falling into the water-tank if one missed one's hold. Finally, the stable itself was the training-ground for the household kittens.

It was not a kitten, however, but a dog that so nearly terminated his career. There must have been thirty or forty mice in the corn-bin at the time. The lid was suddenly flung open, their eyes were dazzled by the blaze of an upheld lantern, and, before they could realize their position, a terrier was amongst them, dealing out scientific murder. Fortunately, he, with one companion, had been where the corn was highest, and a frantic scramble had landed them over the edge of the bin and down behind it. But, from where he lay, he could hear plainly enough what was happening. The mice were leaping in every direction against the polished sides of the bin, missing their footing and falling back into the terrier's mouth. His final recollection was of five and twenty small corpses laid out in a neat row upon the stable floor. Perhaps half a dozen of his companions had escaped by burrowing in the corn.

* * * * *

He awoke with a start this time, for the trap had suddenly turned up on end. The door was standing open, but a shadow hung across it, and the mouse felt the shadow--and shrieked.

THE STORY OF A FIELD VOLE

His earliest recollections were somewhat confused, nor is this to be wondered at, for he was one of eight, and in the same hole lived another family of seven, fifteen tiny creatures in all, of the same age and outwardly indistinguishable.

Under such circumstances it is difficult to retain one's individuality, let alone one's impressions. Moreover some little time had elapsed before he really saw his companions. Not that he was long actually blind,--that is the prerogative of the carnivora, but his career commenced some feet below the surface of the earth, at the termination of a long winding burrow, and a full fortnight had elapsed before he eluded his mother's vigilance, and, after a clumsy scrambling ascent, beheld for the first time the tall green grasses which shrouded the entrance, and the blue of the sky peeping down irregularly between them.

His first sensation was one of extreme cold, for his fur was at this time little better than down; Nature's brilliant colouring only dazzled and frightened him; his tender skin shrank from contact with the sharp-edged herbage, and, after a short blundering excursion, he was glad to scuttle down below once more.

His next effort was more successful. His fur had thickened, and, like all good voles, he had the sense to defer his exit until the evening. Still, even when he had reached the mature age of three weeks, the murky, warm atmosphere below ground proved more seductive than any other, and he spent the greater portion of his existence there, sleeping, nest-making, or fighting with a companion over food.

The making and re-making of the nest was learnt on kindergarten principles. At first he was employed in softening slender grass filaments, by dragging them through his teeth; then he learnt to intertwine them, and sat in the middle of an ever-growing sphere of delicate network; finally, like his mother, he tackled large, stiff grass stems, biting them into short lengths, and splitting them, or letting them split themselves, lengthways. By the time he was a month old, he was an expert nest-builder, and, given the material, could build a complete nest for two inside the hour.

On the score of meat and drink he had no anxieties. A marshy meadow had been selected by his forbears for colonization. The burrow terminated outwardly on the bank of a half-dried watercourse, and, within its recesses, was all manner of vegetable store--seeds, bulbs, leaves, clover, and herbs in fascinating variety and profusion. Nor was there any lack of greener food. Bog-grass surrounded the burrow, and the most succulent portion of bog-grass is the most easily attained.

He soon learned to reach up on his hind legs and gnaw the standing plant. The management of a dry and slippery corn-ear at first presented some difficulty, but, as his muscles strengthened, he found himself able to sit up on his haunches and hold it squirrel-fashion in his fore-paws, nibbling, to begin with, at the pointed end, which is the best way into most things. Once, as the family were grubbing together, a nut turned up at the back of the pile. After a desperate conflict, he secured it, but, the tough shell was too much for him. It takes a red vole's training to reduce a nut.

So the weeks passed on, and he grew thicker and sturdier and more furry. He was never graceful, like his cousin the red vole, for his face was blunted, his eyes small, and his tail ridiculously insignificant. Nor could he cover the ground with the easy swinging jump that makes one suspect relationship between the red vole and the wood-mouse. Still for a common, vulgar, agrarian vole, he was passable enough, and could hold his own, tooth and nail, with his nest-fellows.

He was five weeks old before he commenced to go out foraging on his own account. He never ventured far, but contented himself with timorous excursions along the banks of the watercourse, crouching amid the undergrowth, and ready, at the first scent of danger, to glide with flattened body back to cover. Sometimes he accompanied his mother on her visits to distant portions of the colony, but the old vole more often left her octet behind, and then he would lie huddled up with his companions, waiting for the squelching sound of her footsteps, as she returned across the mud, and quarrelling in anticipation of what she would bring.

Now and again a different sound would reach the hollow--the dragging tail swish of the water-vole, or the fussy scramble of some belated moorhen. These he soon learned to distinguish from the stealthy, broken, hanging footfall of the beast of prey. When that was heard, both he and his companions would crouch together in the darkest corner of the burrow and hold their breath.

Once such a sound stopped abruptly and close at hand; a faint foetid odour permeated from without, and he felt instinctively that the enemy was at the gate. The danger passed, but that night the old vole failed to return.

The night following the same sound came, and ceased. This time, however, the silence was succeeded by a fierce scratching, and he soon realized that the entrance to the nest was blocked, and that something, bigger and stronger than he yet knew of, was working its way nearer and nearer. There was a clatter of falling stones and earth, and the "something" was whirling in their midst. Wild confusion followed. The whole interior of the nest seemed occupied by a swift-circling, curling, sinuous form.

Small as he was, and crouching as only a vole can crouch, there was no escape from contact with it. Three times the hot loathsome breath hissed over him, as he lay flattened to the ground. Then, as the lithe body swept round, he was flung aside, and, by a lucky chance, found himself opposite the outlet. In an agony of terror he scrambled up the shaft, and concealed himself in an adjoining grass-tuft. He was sick, and dizzy, and bruised all over.

Scarcely had he recovered sufficient coolness to look about him, when the object of his terror emerged with dripping jaws, and he was enabled, for the first time, to form an opinion of the arch-enemy of vole-kind.

To avoid the bird of prey, a vole need only remain below the surface; to avoid the little gentleman in black, he need only rise above it; but from the grim pursuit of the weasel, bent on meal or murder, there is no escape.

Terror-stricken as he was, he could hardly help admiring the easy supple swagger of the creature's movements. She held her broad browed head erect, the bristles pointed like needles from her blood-streaked muzzle, grit and pluck could be traced in her every movement, and, in her eyes, universal defiance.

Down the dark watercourse she went, twisting her lithe chestnut body S-wise in and out of the coarse grass-clumps. A frog leaped before her. In a flash she had flung herself upon it, her white teeth clicked together in its brain, and she sauntered slowly out of sight, bearing her latest victim in her mouth. It was hideous. To eat vegetables was natural enough, but to eat living, quivering flesh! A sickening faintness crept over him, and it was full an hour before he could leave his shelter.

Very cautiously he retraced his steps to the familiar entrance, and stopped to listen. A flood of moonlight burst through the clouds, and his trembling shadow danced ink-black before him. He was a clear mark for every kind of foe, yet he still paused irresolute. It was too horribly silent below. A clumsy whirring beetle alighted at his feet and stumbled heavily down the hole. Another followed. He turned and fled, blindly, recklessly, anywhere to escape that exhaling reek of murder.

Away from the watercourse the grasses grew shorter and more slender. It was easy, but risky going. Small pyramids of soil dotted the ground in different directions, some massed together almost in circles, others at wider intervals. At the edge of one of them he stopped and commenced idly burrowing with his fore feet. For a few inches the light, crumbling earth yielded easily to his efforts. Then the floor seemed to subside beneath him, and he found a shelter ready made. Two narrow rough-hewn tunnels led from beneath the centre of the heap. He rested for a few minutes, then started to explore one of them.

It could hardly be described as a burrow, for, at intervals, it was half choked with earth-falls, and he had to work his way through them. In direction it was fairly straight. After a few yards progress he found its termination. It opened on a larger tunnel running at right angles to itself.

The sides of this latter were smooth and polished, smoother even than those of the approach to the old home. It was wide enough for two voles to run abreast in. The straggling grass-roots which hung overhead proved it of trifling depth. Indeed, the roof was very thin, in places hardly solid. Through these the moonlight seemed to filter down, forming dull bluish patches on the floor.

From the main road passages branched out at intervals. He turned into one of them. The sides were rough and crumbling, and it came abruptly to an end. He soon retraced his steps, but paused when he had regained the meeting of the ways. Something was approaching along the main tunnel. He took the wisest course, and crouched within the shelter of the side gallery. A crimson pointed snout, a huge paddling foot, and a dark shapeless mass passed in quick succession before his eyes, and vanished in the darkness.

As it swept by, the foot caught the crumbling edge of his retreat, covering him with a shower of light mould. For the second time he experienced the sickening, paralyzing agony of fear. This was succeeded by an irresistible impulse to break cover. He sprang into the main shaft once more, determined to take advantage of the first outlet. A shadowy blue glimmer shone before him, and he quickened his pace towards it. Suddenly the light was extinguished, the walls of the tunnel seemed to cave in around him, in front of him he heard a dull, choking gasp, and he found his nose in contact with a warm, palpitating velvet body.

This time his nerve failed him completely, and he lay absolutely motionless, conscious, with only a dull indifference, that death stared him in the face. But death seemed slow in coming, and, as he lay, his indifference changed to a fierce longing, first for a speedy end of it all, then for life at any price. Slowly and with difficulty he lifted his head; the dark mass lay silent alongside of him, and the faint movements had ceased. He could trace the creature's hind foot, it was rigid and cold. Then the truth burst upon him. He had nothing to fear--the owner of the foot was dead.

Still, he could scarcely move his limbs, for the soil lay thick and heavy around him. After a prolonged effort he disengaged his fore feet, and started to scratch himself free. On one side of him lay the dead body; he worked vigorously along it. He was checked, however, by an obstacle beyond his strength. The body was enclosed by a tight-fitting ring, and on this he could make no impression.

Fastening his tiny fingers in the fur on one side, and scraping with his free fore-paw on the other, he forced his way upwards. The soil grew lighter above him, and in a few minutes he had reached the upper air, and lay panting on the surface.

He then tried to pick up his position. The mole-run had brought him some two hundred yards, nearly to the edge of the marshland. Across the boundary rose a small plantation. Here he determined to seek shelter. He had but fifty yards to go, and started to glide stealthily from tuft to tuft.

On all sides the ground was alive with tiny insects. The larger kinds seemed mostly to be sleeping. He ran full tilt against a drowsy butterfly, sweeping its close-folded wings through half a circle, as he passed. They sprang back with a jerk, but the insect itself remained motionless. Grasshoppers clung to every other grass-stem; their eyes were dead and staring. Here and there he saw a spider gripping its support and waiting for the sunrise.

Once he found himself confronted by a bloated toad. The amphibian surveyed him solemnly, but never moved. A low hiss whistled through the grass. He crouched in terror while four feet of grass-snake undulated by. A shrewmouse broke cover in front of him, followed by its mate. The air resounded with shrill defiant squeaks as the two bunchy velvet balls rolled over one another out of sight.

So he worked his way along towards the boundary; pausing at intervals to gnaw at the growing plant-stems, or to sit on his haunches and nibble some fallen seed which took his fancy.

It was close to the plantation that a familiar movement in the grass seemed to betray the presence of a near relation. Hastening towards it he found himself confronted by a total stranger. Vole-like this latter undoubtedly was, yet he was no ordinary vole. Delicate chestnut fur, brilliant white feet, a whitish waistcoat, and a paste-coloured two-inch tail proclaimed the red vole at once.

In size there was little to choose between them, and they sat gazing at each other for some moments stolid and undismayed. Yet, despite the equality of fighting weight, he felt himself somehow the inferior creature. His thoughts ran on the old legend of the field-vole who mated with a wood-mouse of high degree, and whose descendants to this day bear the marks of their noble origin. So, when the stranger turned and leapt lightly into the undergrowth that fringed the wood, he humbly tried to follow.

That was no easy matter, for, where the other jumped, he could only scramble, and on the flat he felt himself hopelessly outclassed. Still, once beyond the outskirts of the wood, the tangled thickets gave way to something less luxuriant, and he could sight his leader more frequently. All at once he checked himself, and, with a sudden access of natural caution, flattened himself to earth. He had blundered into the red-vole community.

Five small active forms were gliding hither and thither among the fallen leaves. They were too busy to notice him, and were evidently working with some method, for, at intervals, one or the other would make his way slowly to a definite spot, and then return light-footed to his task. He edged a little closer to observe them. Then the meaning of it flashed upon him. They were nut-hunting.

Sometimes the nut was carried in their mouths, sometimes rolled along the ground, sometimes wedged between the chin and fore-paws, but, when they reached their goal, it seemed to vanish.

Of this there could be but one solution. The nuts were being taken to a burrow-entrance. Curiosity overcame him, and, seizing a quiet moment, he slipped down the burrow. It plunged abruptly for about a foot, passed under a curving root, squeezed between some small root branches, and terminated in a double compartment. Three nuts hit him from behind as he descended.

To his left lay the nest, a mass of feathery grass and mosses. He slipped into it, and, as he cleared the shaft entrance, the three nuts followed with a rush. He lay there quiet until his eyes had become accustomed to the semi-darkness.

Then he perceived that he was not alone. The right-hand portion of the hollow held a lady tenant. She had her back to him, and was busily employed in the storeroom. He could just distinguish that the farthest recess held a great pile of nuts, and that her business was to collect the nuts as they toppled down the shoot, and stack them in as small a space as possible.

Suddenly she paused, and he saw her sniff suspiciously, she swung round, and he was discovered. He had barely time to back into a corner, before she was upon him, and at the first nip, he knew that he had met a better vole. Over they rolled, scratching, biting, tearing. Her sharp, chisel teeth met in his ear and tore the half of it away. The blood blinded him, but he stuck grimly to his task.

Physically he was at an immense disadvantage. His clumsy movements availed but little against the fierce agility of the red vole. Time after time he snapped at her and missed; for, even as he aimed, she could swing her lithe body round and leap upon him from behind. Nor, when they grappled, could he retain his hold on her. Against the leverage of those powerful hind legs he could do nothing.

His cause, moreover, was a bad one. Was he not the intruder? and when was ever mercy accorded to such among four-footed things? His strength was fast failing when he fled, hotly pursued, up to the open once more. He only exchanged one foe for four. Lacerated, faint, and bleeding, he crouched, waiting for their attack. It was a short and savage one. An owl hooted above, the red voles rushed to cover, but he remained behind.

He had only really felt one bite. A pair of razor teeth had nipped his spine, and--he had hardly noticed a dozen other wounds. He was terribly thirsty, and struggled to reach a dewdrop which hung above his head, but his hind legs were paralyzed and powerless. Gradually his eyelids drooped, and he sank slowly over on one side. It was growing very dark and very cold.

THE APOLOGY OF THE HOUSE SPARROW

(NOTE.--It would not be morally profitable to describe how I learnt Sparrowese. The language of the sparrow is the language of the gutter. I have Englishized it throughout.)

"I was the odd egg, for one thing," said the sparrow. He was speaking with his mouth full, as usual.

"What on earth do you mean by that?" I replied.

He laughed offensively. "Do you know anything about sparrows?" he sneered.

I confessed I did not know much.

"I never knew any one write about them who did," he went on. "What was I saying when you interrupted me?"

"You said you were the odd egg," I replied. "What is an odd egg?"

"Do you know what a clutch is?" His intonation was insolence itself.

"A clutch," said I, "is, I believe, a sitting of eggs destined to be simultaneously hatched."

"Perhaps you may have noticed," said he, "that in our family"--his every feather bristled with importance, and the white bars on his wings were beautifully displayed--"we do not confine ourselves to a single monotonous pattern of egg."

"A string of variegated sparrows' eggs was one of my earliest treasures," said I.

"Well, then, if you know that much, and don't know what the odd egg is, you must be a fool," said he.

It is hard to be insulted by a sparrow, and, as it is, I have toned down the expression, but I preserved a meek silence.

"Any one," he went on, with bland condescension, "who has seen a few clutches of sparrows' eggs, and has not noticed that there is an odd egg in each clutch, must be an uncommonly poor observer."

"It is not in the books," I ventured to protest.

"Books!" he screamed, "books! What do the people who write books know about sparrows? And yet, do you know that there has been more ink spilt over sparrows than over any other bird? that laws innumerable have been passed concerning sparrows? that associations have been formed to exterminate sparrows? that--that--that----"

The excitement was too much for him; he had been keeping time with his tail to this declamatory crescendo. With the last effort he cocked it a shade too high, lost his balance, and landed, considerably ruffled, some four feet beneath his own reserved and particular twig. His eye was on me, and I felt it too serious a matter for laughter. He made what was evidently intended for a dignified ascent, choosing, with minute exactness, the steps he had originally employed on my approach. It was a full minute before he broke the silence, and for that full minute I had to preserve my gravity.

"Have you any clutches by you?" he said at last.

I had, and fetched them.

"Now," said he, "look at that one, four dark and one light; look at this, four light and one dark; and at this, six light mottled, and one among them with a few black spots."

I had to admit that it seemed true.

"True," said he, "of course it's true. Didn't I tell you that I was the odd egg myself?"

"Well, one of you had to be the odd egg, I suppose?"

"Wrong again," said he. "What you don't seem to realize is, that the odd egg is nearly always addled; in my case it wasn't."

"Then, in your case," said I, "there was one more mouth to feed than your parents expected. How did they take it?"

"Mother kept it quiet as long as she could," said he.

"And father?"

"Father didn't find out for a day or two, and when he did, he pushed one of my brothers over the side of the nest--he did holler for his life!"

The little beast was actually chuckling at the recollection.

"He hung head downwards by one leg, and wouldn't let go till father dug his beak into him."

"Brutal," I murmured.

"Brutal! not a bit of it. You can't feed more than a certain number of nestlings; besides which, there wouldn't be room in the nest. As it was, I fell out before I could fly."

"What happened then?"

"Why, the old folks came and fed me, and helped me back again the shortest way up the bark. Brutal, wasn't it? A martin wouldn't do that."

"Which reminds me," said I, "that you were not born in a martin's-nest. Are trees the fashionable quarter just now?"

"They've come in more since thatched roofs went out," said the sparrow. "It's tree or martins'-nests nowadays."

"You do really drive away the martins, I suppose?"

"Yes," he sniggered; "poor, dear little martins! Look here," said he, and his voice changed from a snigger to vicious earnest. "We sparrows are just about sick of being accused of bullying martins. White of Selborne started it, but he didn't know what it would lead to. Would you like to know the truth of the matter?"

It was one of the things I did want to hear, and I nodded assent.

"The disappearance of martins is a loss really of national importance," he began, in a sickly whine. "It is a shame to see how the pretty house martins are decreasing in this country at the hand of the sparrows," he continued. "He drives away our migratory and pre-eminently useful insect-eating birds, even turning out the eggs of the owners and using the locality for its own nest."

He was obviously quoting from the pro-martin authorities, and I stopped him.

"I have heard all that before," said I.

"There's a fair amount of it about, pages and pages," said he; "there's one story, for instance, of twenty or thirty martins blocking up the bold, bad sparrow inside the nest, which the said bold, bad sparrow had usurped. What do you think of that?"

"I think it is untrue," I promptly replied.

"It is untrue," said he; "but it isn't far away from truth, for all that. Many a dead sparrow has been found in a martin's-nest, and many a time the entrance was too small for a sparrow to have got out of; but, still, it wouldn't take a healthy sparrow long to break up a martin's-nest."

"What has happened then?" said I.

"Why, of course, the sparrow was dying when it got in. One part of white arsenic to fifteen parts of corn-meal is the usual recipe. It is illegal, as you doubtless know, but it has the advantage of acting slowly. Of course, if we saw a friend of ours writhing about in the feeding-ground, we should give that feeding-ground a wide berth."

"I see," said I; "but what about the entrance being plastered up?"

"It is never quite plastered up," said he; "and even if it was, a healthy, able-bodied sparrow could knock the whole thing to pieces with two pecks. No; when there are any disputes as to proprietorship between sparrows and martins, the martins have a trick of waiting till the sparrow is out, and then narrowing down the entrance so that the sparrow will have a job to get in decent nest material. When a live sparrow is in possession, he very soon lets callers know it. The martins, in these cases, miss their usual greeting, and probably conclude that the sparrow is away, whereas he is really dead inside. That's just about the whole truth of the matter."

"But why on earth," I protested, "can't you build a proper nest for yourself?"

"I don't know why it is," said he, "but the mere thought of a martin makes a sparrow feel bad inside. Why does a dog naturally go for a cat? One thing is quite certain, however. We both fancy human dwellings, and, if we left the martins altogether alone, they would have all the best places in no time. Now, that wouldn't be fair at all. I appeal to you as a fellow Briton. We are British born and bred. We stay with you all the year round. The martin only comes to look you up in the fine weather. Then he puts on his showy foreign manners, and you say, 'How charming! so different to those dirty, vulgar sparrows!' but, as soon as the weather breaks, off he goes. Now, a hard winter is no fun for the sparrows. We are glad of any shelter we can get, and the martins' deserted nests come in very handy. Not only do we use them, but we keep them from falling to pieces, line them with feathers, and make them into snug winter quarters. Back comes the martin in the spring. 'Dear me!' he says, 'most gratifying, I am sure. So kind of you to act as caretaker. Why, I declare, the old place looks better than when I left. Of course, you won't mind my coming in at once. I've got to make my family arrangements for the season.' 'Not quite,' says the sparrow. 'If it hadn't been for me, this nest would have been down in the last gale. I've put money into this nest, and you can jolly well go and build another. You ought to have stayed to look after it, if you wanted it again.'"

"That is all very well," said I; "but it seems to me that there ought to be room for both of you."

"Well, there isn't," said he, "and Nature has worked it out that there shan't be, and if you write a thousand letters to the Field, you won't alter that."

"Suppose the martins got the pull over the sparrows, do you think it would be better for things in general?"

"You mean better for yourself," said the sparrow, sharply.

On reflection, I came to the conclusion that that was just what I did mean.

"I don't believe an increase of insect-eating birds would do you much good," he went on. "Suppose, for instance, the ichneumon flies were decimated, what a time it would be for the caterpillars! How would some of your plants get on if there weren't enough insects to fertilize them?"

I felt it was time to shift my ground. "Let us get back to your early history," said I. "What was the nest like?"

"It was in a hole of a tree-stump," said he. "A silly sort of place, I think, not ten feet from the ground. Now I always build as high as I can--just underneath the rooks'-nests, in fact. You're safe from boys; they don't shoot your nest to bits for fear of shooting the rooks'-nests too; and there's abundance of insect food on the spot. The nest itself was mostly feathery stuff, though I remember a piece of pink paper, which used to tickle me. I suppose the colour of it took the old birds' fancy. Of course the nest was distinct from the casing. That was the usual straw. I think it is the casing of sparrows'-nests that you humans object to as untidy."

"We chiefly object to the portion which stops up the water-pipes," said I. "What did you have to eat?"

"Insects, I expect, to start with. At least, that is what I always give my youngsters; then, as my gizzard strengthened, small, hard seeds; then bigger ones; finally, corn itself. That is my favourite diet at the present time. Three parts of what I eat is corn, the rest is insects, seeds, and scraps."

"You can get corn all the year round?"

"Oh! easily enough. In the fields, when it is growing; round the wheat-stacks later, or among the poultry--people don't shoot into the middle of the poultry--anywhere, in fact."

"And you really like corn better than anything?"

"There is nothing quite so nice in the world," said the sparrow, "as fresh, young corn in the ear, which you can just squeeze the juice out of and then drop."

"And are you aware of the amount of damage which you do to the poor, struggling farmer?" said I, assuming a judicial severity which I was far from feeling.

The flippancy was infectious.

"A recent estimate places it at ?70,094 per annum," said the sparrow. "Just think of that!"

"In this country alone," said I. "You seem to forget America, Australia, South Africa, and all the other places to which you have been unhappily introduced as an insecticide."

"You seem to forget," he retorted, "that it was you yourselves who made the introduction. You tried to improve on the natural balance which was ordained for this string of countries, and a pretty mess you have made of it. Now you want to crown your folly of introducing the sparrow where Nature said it was not wanted, by exterminating it where Nature says it is wanted--and that's here."

"I don't think any one has suggested that you should be exterminated," said I.

"'To lessen their numbers in our country, every possible means must be had recourse to.' There's a pretty piece of grammar for you."

He was obviously quoting again.

"You couldn't exterminate me if you tried, and, therefore, you very properly don't suggest it. I have been called the Avian Rat, and I am the Avian Rat. You can no more get rid of me than you can of my four-footed counterpart. It would be a bad day for you if you could."

"But you must admit that both you and the rat are increasing in numbers, and, therefore, in destructiveness. What is to be the end of it?"

"The end of it will be that you will preserve our enemies instead of shooting them at sight."

"Meaning?"

"Hawks, owls, weasels, and so on."

"But hawks would never come near the towns?"

"We aren't in town the whole year round. Even the cockneyest of sparrows has his month or two in the cornfields. I don't mind telling you that one of the reasons we have for clinging to human habitations is that we are thus sure of sanctuary. Our natural enemies will always be welcomed with a gun. They know that, too, and keep away. Make it an offence to kill a bird or beast of prey, and you will see a difference in the rats and sparrows."

"What about the pheasants?" said I.

"There would be fewer pheasants," said the sparrow; "and, if you only knew it, they would taste better, if there were."

"Sparrow," said I, "to speak disrespectfully of the battue places you at once outside the pale. You are an Avian Rat. You do consume an inordinate quantity of corn. Since history began you have been an impudent parasite on man. As a hieroglyphic character you signified the enemy. Choleric old gentlemen have been roused to frenzy over your misdeeds. You have been shot at, trapped, poisoned, netted. Like the chafers, you have been excommunicated. You have been made into a yearly tribute, by the thousand. Laws have been enacted to compass your destruction, letters have been written to the Field, and yet--and yet--an inscrutable Providence has decreed that you shall survive, increase, and multiply. What good do you do?"

"Have you ever heard me sing?" said the sparrow.

"Sing!" I cried; "that sempiternal twitter, that intolerable chirrup that destroys the best and latest hours of sleep! Do you call that singing?"

"What bird would you prefer?" he blandly inquired.

I considered for a moment. The grim possibility of ten thousand nightingales yodelling in chorus, of ten thousand skylarks, or of ten thousand cuckoos, determined my answer.

"I cannot think of one," said I. "But this is no merit on your part, it is merely a qualification of evil."

"I thought you would acknowledge that," said the sparrow. "But, seriously, you ask me what good I do, and I will tell you. That my infant food consisted entirely of insects and caterpillars you already know. Turn the statistician to work who has so cunningly reduced my corn-depredations to pounds, shillings, and pence, and he will assuredly find that the insects devoured by the infant sparrow population in a year will amount to hundreds of millions. These, mind you, are insects large enough to be brought to us in our parent's beaks.

"But what of the insect eggs devoured by us in winter, when most of your pretty insect-eating birds have flown to where the insect is commoner, fatter, and fuller-flavoured? It is we stay-at-home British birds that really keep the insects down. I know that insect eggs do not appear in our poor dissected gizzards. How should they? How would you recognize their remains, O sapient sparrow-shooters? But they are there, for all that. Those blessed with eyes can see us hunting for them in the fallen leaves, among the garbage, in the crannies of the very pavement.

"What, again, of weed seeds in general, and knotgrass in particular? Avian Rat, indeed! rather Avian Scavenger, who draws his hard-earned pay in corn. Can you grudge him a few paltry millions? Would you exterminate him because in your blindness you only note the debit side? There is a Power behind the sparrow. It is Nature herself, and against Her fixed resolve nothing avails."

He had worked himself into an incoherent frenzy; but, even as he relapsed from this fierce air of consequence to his vulgarian self, I felt ashamed.

THE AWAKENING OF THE DORMOUSE

He lay face downwards--two tiny fists tight-clenched against his cheeks, his feet curled up to meet them, his tail swung gracefully across his eyes.

Nine weeks had he lain thus, self-entombed. Within the hollow of the old hazel-stump he had fashioned a rough sphere of honeysuckle bark; within this, again, a nest of feathery grass stems. He had put the roof on last of all.

A winter sunbeam pierced the screen of woodbine, and, for a moment, shed the warmth of springtime on the nest. His whiskers gave a feeble flicker in response. Next day the treacherous radiance lingered. He unclenched one fist, and wound four tiny fingers round a grass-stem. On the fourth day he half-opened his eyes (even half-opened they were beautiful), and sat up, dazed and blinking. The sunbeam had reached his heart.

Yet it was a full hour before he was conscious that he lived. At first he felt nothing but a dull quickening throb within his body. His feet and hands were ice-cold, and he swayed from side to side, feeling for his strength. Then came the pricking of ten thousand tiny needles in his limbs. His heart beat as though it would burst its prison. His whole frame quivered. His bristles stood stiff-pointed from their roots. As the heart-throb slowed, his muscles slackened and obeyed his will, but yet he felt that something was amiss. Before him danced a yellow quivering haze, his feet were heavy and awkward, his chest ached as he breathed, and he was cold, oh, so cold! It was no easy matter to reach the nest-top. He climbed mechanically upwards, digging his toes into the meshwork of the sides, and sobbing from sheer weakness as he climbed.

He made a small parting in the roof, and peeped out. It was only for a moment, for he fell back stunned and blinded by the glare. Still, in that moment, he had caught a glimpse of an unfamiliar world, leafless, lifeless, silent, miserable. He tucked his nose between his four paws, swung his tail across his eyes, and waited patiently for the darkness. With the darkness came the cold. It stole upon him gently, quelled the heart-throb, reclenched the tiny fists, and lulled him to forget.

* * * * *

It was better the next time. The old hazel was making coquettish efforts to renew its youth. It had hung its last remaining shoot with dancing catkins. Here and there lurked a crimson bud, ready to catch the floating pollen. On the sloping banks below were splotches of violet and primrose, and, over all, hung the green shimmer of spring.

To the dormouse's eyes the glare was, for the first few moments, as painful as before, but this time it was tempered with moisture. Great rain-drops swung on the swaying grass-stems and twinkled with a thousand prismatic colours. The slow drip of the woods resounded in his ears.

As his hearing sharpened, the old familiar sounds returned, the chirping of the titmice, the starling's discord, the sniggering of the robin, the squirrel's bullying cough. How he had hated the squirrel--a midget incarnation of mischief, whose whole life was spent in practical joking. How often had he heard that hateful cough shot into his ear, as My Lady Shadowtail whisked past him, a sinuous brown flash curling round the tree trunk! How often had he promptly dropped his hard-earned nut in consequence, only to see it seized by a field-mouse! How often had he swung at the end of a tapering twig, while the squirrel feinted at him with all four paws!

He looked up, and caught the squirrel's eye.

"What, awake?" she shouted. "It's not quite time for good little dormice. You wait till it's dark, and see how cool it is. Why, even with my tail (and she bent it into a figure of eight to show its amplitude) it is hard enough to keep warm."

"Chuc!"

The dormouse had felt it coming, and had discreetly retired. As it was, the better part of the roof caved in, the result of slight mistiming on the part of the squirrel.

"I wish you wouldn't do that," said the dormouse.

He was addressing vacancy, for the squirrel had in the mean time completed the circuit of three tree-tops. She was back again, however, in time to catch the next remark.

"Have you any nuts?" said the dormouse. "I feel most horribly hungry, and this light is very trying to my eyes. It will have to be darker before I can hunt for any myself."

"You'll be asleep two hours before it's dark," said the squirrel, "and I haven't any nuts, or rather, I haven't the least idea where I put them. Didn't you make a store?"

"Only a small one--seeds, I think," said the dormouse. "I was very drowsy when I made it, and I daren't hope that it is in good order."

"Where is it?" said the squirrel.

"The second hazel on the left," said the dormouse; "the third hollow from the top."

The second hazel on the left was twenty yards away. Before the dormouse had finished speaking the squirrel had started, and the boughs by which she reached it were still quivering as she returned.

"There's your store."

The dormouse looked up, and gave a dolorous squeal of disappointment. A straggling nosegay was being thrust through the roof, and he realized at once that the seeds had sprouted.

"Why didn't you nibble the ends off?" said the squirrel. "You can't expect seeds to be seeds for ever. Oh, it's your first hibernation, is it? Well, you'll know better next time. Here's a nut for you." She had held it concealed in her palm, and produced it like a conjuror.

"She's not such a bad sort, after all," thought the dormouse, as he proceeded to examine the nut.

It was a hard nut, and would take some getting through. He sat back on his haunches, grasped it in his eight little fingers, gave it a twirl or two, and commenced gnawing three strokes a second. He gnawed for two minutes without a break.

It was harder than any other nut he remembered. He had never been more than a minute getting through one; sometimes they had obligingly split in half before he had fairly started. He tried another part, and worked even more vigorously than before.

Assuredly it was the very hardest nut in all the world. Twenty minutes' hard work produced a small round hole, ten minutes more enlarged it so that he could thrust his lips inside. Then he sucked vigorously to secure the kernel, and secured instead a mouthful of black dust.

Of course the squirrel had known it all along. It did not need the guffaw he heard above to tell him that. This time he did not even protest. His spirit was broken. He was cold and tired and hungry. He merely huddled in a corner, still grasping the nut, and breathing in queer short gasps.

"Never mind, dormouse," shouted the squirrel, "you will know a bad egg next time. Try this."

For five seconds there was a faint rasping sound, then a sharp crack, and the rustle of two half-nutshells through the leaves. One of them struck the side of the hazel-stump and bounded off like an elastic ball. Before the dormouse had collected his wits, a fine kernel was thrust through the nest and the squirrel had once more regained her bough.

"Eat it," she shrieked; "eat it before the sun goes down. It's going now."

And it was. Before a quarter of the kernel was accounted for, the western sky had turned to lurid orange; before the half was gone, the chill struck him. The nut dropped from his nerveless hands, his limbs tightened, his ears sank into his skin, his eyelids drooped, and he was asleep once more.

* * * * *

The primroses had long yielded pride of place to the daffodils; these in turn had paled before the marsh marigolds, but the most glorious yellow in the picture was the Sulphur Butterfly. He zigzagged lightly down the hedgerow, catching the sunshine at every turn, and the marigolds drooped their heads at the sight of him. Close to the nest he dropped on a briar-leaf, like a floating petal. He was more than colour now--he was form. For a full minute he poised there motionless, the most exquisitely graceful, the most exquisitely coloured of all our butterflies, and, for a full minute, the dormouse watched him.

Next came a quivering, amber-tinted flight, resolved at rest into a delicate medley of green and white and saffron. It was the orange-tip, and the dormouse rejoiced, for the orange-tip meant spring. Such dainty frailty could never stand the winter.

To tell of all he heard and saw that day would fill a book. At first, as he peered through the crevices, he only grasped the more vivid tints--the azure of the hyacinth, the roseblush of the almond, the crimson glow of the clover, the purple of the foxglove. Then, as his senses quickened, the whole glorious colour-scale, from ashbud to whitethorn, stood revealed.

From heaven above came the skylark's defiant challenge; from earth beneath the fussy scream of the blackbird; on all sides the tweetings, twitterings, chirrupings, chirrings and pipings of petulant finches, and, in tender modulation to the avian chorus, the deep-throated, innumerable, drowsy hum of insects. Colour and sound, love and war, it was spring indeed.

For the dormouse, one tiny penetrating note dominated all. He knew that the singer of that note was four-footed. Have you ever heard a cricket's serenade? It was something like that. Have you ever heard a tree-creeper talking to itself? It was something like that also. He looked down and saw, as he expected, a round fur ball rolling in and out the grass-stems. At times the ball sat up and sniffed. He knew the puny fists and tapering snout at once. It was the shrewmouse. "Shrewmouse!" he cried, "is it time?" But the shrewmouse had crouched to dodge the shadow of a passing bird, and he saw him no more. However, he had seen enough. He stretched his hands and feet as though he would rack them from their sockets. Like Tennyson's rabbit, he fondled his harmless face in the most elaborate of toilets, then he took one nibble at the remnant of the squirrel's nut, and dropped off to sleep till the twilight.

It is time to describe him.

"Figure somewhat stout," says the book, "a single pair of pre-molars in each jaw, first toe of the fore-foot rudimentary, tail cylindrical," etc. The dormouse was anything but stout--six months' fasting, save for half a nut, had effectually restrained any tendency that way. No doubt in other respects he was in fair accordance with museum pattern, but he differed in one essential particular--he was alive.

His colour? When he had first retired to rest he had closely resembled a young red vole, buff grey all over save for his white waistcoat and the hair-parting along his back and down the ridges of his limbs. This was a delicate auburn. During his sleep the auburn had overspread his back, softened into cream colour on his sides, and thence into a pure white front. Ages ago his ancestors had been white all over; now, amid changed surroundings, the white only lingered where it was least conspicuous.

His eyes? Nor pen nor camera can present them. Imagine a black pearl imprisoning a diamond; imagine a dewdrop trembling on polished jet; add to these beauties life, and you will have the dormouse eye.

His tail? Distichous, say the books. Feathers are mostly distichous, hair-partings are distichous, the moustache is distichous. So is the dormouse tail; but the hairs along it do more than merely part. They curl, upwards from the root, downwards to the point, and form a plume.

The plume is a natural parachute, not so obvious, perhaps, as in the squirrel's case, but, weight for weight, of equal service.

His feet? Ten toes behind and eight before, sharp-pointed toes that grip the slenderest twig, and catch the slightest foothold in the bark.

His ears? Small, say the books. Not small, but rather hidden in the deep surrounding fur.

Had you seen the dormouse at the moment of his final awakening, you might have recognized him from this description. A few minutes later and the grey, flitting shadow might easily have baffled you. For, as he reached the surface of his nest, the sun went down.

Before him, at last, lay the twilight world he loved. Nature had ceased her noise and commenced her melody. From the brook below came the dull plash of the rising trout; now and then one could catch a stealthy rustle in the herbage--the beetles were abroad, ay and the mice and the beasts of prey; a hare paced by with easy lilting stride; his gentle footfall hardly stirred the dust. In the distance sounded the cry of a lost soul. It was the barn owl starting on her rounds. The dormouse cowered back until she passed--white--gleaming, swift and silent as a moth.

There was no discordant note. Wood, meadow, and hedgerow were bathed in liquid blue. The very tree trunks stood out as indigo against the sky. Daisy and marigold, hyacinth and clover were attuned to the same soothing minor chord. The work-a-day world was at rest, but the sleep-a-day world was holding high revel.

Before he was halfway down the stump he had caught the glint of twenty pairs of eyes. The voles and wood-mice had waited, like himself, until the owl had passed. Before each tuft of grass now stood its latest tenant. From beneath the root of a neighbouring hazel came a stealthy procession of five bank voles. Each, as it gained the entrance, performed its normal round. First it sniffed for weasel, then it sat up and washed its face, then it sniffed again, finally it stole off, foraging among the grass-stems. He saw his friend the shrewmouse scuffling with its mate; he saw the wood-mice nut-grubbing; he saw the night reunion of the stump-tailed voles; but the first of his own kind that he saw was mother.

He had swung himself to the top of a broken twig, and, as he looked down, perceived her climbing stiffly up towards him. Mother had aged since the autumn, but, when she drew closer, he knew her well enough; it was the same soft fur that he had nestled in last year.

Together they went out into the night. Once more he felt the magic pulse of life within him, and ran to the top of the hedge and down again twenty times for the mere joy of running. Head upwards he flew, head downwards, backwards, forwards, sideways. Sometimes he paused for a moment, lightly balanced on a branch end, then swung himself to the next friendly projection. Sometimes there was no pause. In one easy unbroken course he travelled to the end, cleared the intervening gap, and landed on the neighbouring branch below. He never missed, he never stumbled; for he was tumbler and wire-walker and saltimbanque in one.

And mother? Mother had lost some of her spring, but she had developed judiciousness, and a fine eye for country. It was this latter which, to her son's amazement, usually kept her two bushes ahead. It was this which made him miss her as the day broke.

He had been to the very topmost pinnacle of a thorn-bush; halfway down he had leapt four feet on to a neighbouring hazel; he had looked back in self-congratulation at the abyss, and, when he had turned again, she had disappeared.

He waited for her as long as he dared, and then crept back subdued and lonely to his nest. Next evening perhaps he would see her again. But the next evening passed, and the next, and the next, and he never saw her again until the end.

Some other time I will tell you how he passed that summer, how he fought for and won a wife, how they built a nest together and made a store together, of the four little dormice, and of the sad fate that befel two of them. Here I can only tell the last scene.

It was late autumn. His wife had already felt the coming of winter, and retired to her six months' sleep. He himself had sealed her in.

He had taught the two small dormice how to build their nests (honeysuckle fibre and dead leaf), and pointed out the necessity of getting into them before Christmas. He had rebuilt his own nest in the same old hollow, for he knew that he could not hold out much longer.

With every light breeze that crept down the hedgerow now came the rustle of the falling leaf. Each night he had seemed less inclined to wake, and this night he seemed less inclined than ever.

The sun had scarcely set before he felt chilled and uncomfortable. To warm himself he did three minutes' gymnastics. The end of them found him perched on the same old broken twig, and, when he looked down, even as before, mother was climbing painfully up to him.

It needed but a glance to see that she would not outlive the winter. Had she made a nest? No, she had not troubled. The hole she was in last year would do. Perhaps she would take his nest, he could easily build another. Most certainly she would not. He could help her to put some leaves into hers to-morrow. But that night came the first frost.

THE PURPLE EMPEROR

Down by the brookside the Sallow drooped her sunburnt leaves despondently. Things were at their dullest.

Three months ago she had been a tree of importance. Her dark, slender branches had formed a fashionable rendez-vous. Each evening she had seen her golden catkins studded with opals--the eyes of soft, furry, blundering moths. Each day the bees had thronged to pay court to her.

Then came Palm Sunday. Her catkins were stripped from her, worn for a few hours in yokels' hats, and flung aside. The moths came no more; the bees forsook her for the bluebells.

But the kingfishers cared nothing for her appearance. They nested, as usual, deep in the bank below, in a hollow formed by her roots.

The kingfishers were always in a hurry, and their colours were fussy and discordant. They flashed up and down the brook like a pair of demented fireworks. The whole bank reeked with the discarded meals of their progeny.

By the time the nestlings were fledged, the sallow wore its summer mantle, a down-lined cloak of green.

The interesting event had been a diversion. Now there seemed nothing to look forward to.

On the one side lay the meadow-land, stretching in unbroken monotony to the sky-line; on the other, the brook; beyond its wooded bank, more meadow-land.

The brook was not what it had been. Its waters were being drawn away to thirsty London, and herein lay the sallow's chief vexation.

This year her upper boughs had never flowered. Summer arrived, and she had hoped against hope. They had never even put forth leaves.

To be prematurely bald is disheartening. This baldness was so premature as to be serious. It was the first warning of decay.

* * * * *

The Empress Mother came sailing over the hill, high in the sky as befitted her. Behind her, in the far distance, lay the white-ribbed downs, and, along their ridge, there stretched against the sky a thin, shadowy, broken line. It was the great oak wood, the dominion she had abandoned.

The Empress Mother was looking for a black sallow. Sallows there were in plenty in and about the great wood, but she wanted one all to herself; one fit for an imperial nursery. So she came with unerring instinct to the brook.

The air hung motionless in the grip of a midsummer noon. As she floated earthwards in stately majesty, the sunlight flung its radiance round her, and her broad, white ribbon gleamed on its velvet ground like molten silver.

The sallow humbly drooped her leaves as one who receives royalty.

For an hour the Empress Mother was busy. The leaves that she honoured were chosen with the nicest discrimination, and she honoured more than a dozen. Each, as she left it, bore on its upper surface a small, green-yellow, shiny, translucent cone, rounded at the top, flat at the base, and ribbed along its sides.

For the rest of the day the sallow held her head high.

* * * * *

There were fourteen eggs in all. Six reached maturity, but we are only concerned with one of them. Outwardly he was much like the others. A day's exposure softened the yellow of his shell to olive. Save at the base he matched his leaf surroundings to a nicety. The base was suffused with a faint blush of purple. As the days passed the purple darkened to black, and shifted upwards, leaving the parts beneath it pale and colourless. It seemed to struggle towards the sun. On the eighteenth day the shell parted at the summit, and the little Emperor was hatched.

His youthful Majesty was mostly dark brown head. Such body as he could boast of was tapering and greenish. But his head caught the eye. It was well-nigh as large as the egg from which he came. Until he had fed he seemed indifferent to his changed surroundings.

The first thing that he ate was his minute discarded shell, and, from this slender meal, resulted disproportionate energy. He started forthwith on his travels, outwards towards the light as far as he could go. On the leaf point he built himself a pigmy throne of silk; and this was his citadel for a week. He only left it to feed, nibbling the leaf edge jerkily on either side of him. At the week's end he lost his appetite. His body was now of a decided green--green with the finest powdering of yellow. About his waist the yellow fused into a crescent. Nine of him would have measured an inch.

On the eighth day he ceased feeding altogether. He sat with his hind-quarters anchored to his throne, his head and fore legs raised from off the leaf, rigid and immovable. For three days he grew yellower and yellower. Then his skin split down his back, and he successfully accomplished his first moult. In his short span he passed through many changes, but never one more quaint than this.

During his abstinence he had grown two horns. They branched straight out before him, bristling with short spines, a full third of his length.

He moulted once again before the winter, but this was merely a growing moult. Until October he never left his leaf point. Then Nature herself warned him to seek shelter. The weather was breaking. Rain he did not mind, but wind was different. Suppose his leaf was torn from its socket and hurled a hundred yards into the field?

Leaves were falling all round him, and it was time to take up his winter quarters. He spent a day or two in reaching them, yet they were not far off--merely the junction of his own particular branch to the parent stem. There, in the shelter of the fork, he spun himself a silken blanket, and in it he slept peacefully till April.

Peacefully through everything, and in spite of everything. Rain beat in drenching floods against the sallow, hailstorms lashed her branches, snow enshrouded her, hoar-frost bespangled her,-- the little Emperor was quite unmoved. As the bark weathered from ebony to rusty olive, chameleon-like, he changed with it. This was the only outward sign he gave of life.

* * * * *

The catkins bloomed once more, and once more were rudely gathered. With the bursting of the leaf the little Emperor crept from his blanket. He found the world much as he had left it. Only the leaves were covered with soft down, smaller, and easier to bite. He was by now a full half inch in length, big enough to roam at large, and hungry enough to eat the tree. He started on the first leaf he came to, and, in five minutes, had gnawed a neat crescent out of it. There was method in his gnawing. He fixed his claspers firmly to the stalk, then stretched his head as far as he could reach, and nibbled the leaf edge backwards. When his feet reached his claspers, he commenced afresh.

Before the winter he had only fed at night; now he fed from sunrise to sunset, and at night as well. He fattened steadily, and in proportion, growing more slug-like every day. His horns but emphasized the likeness. He carried them well forward, and, at his rare sleeping intervals, they lay flat against the leaf. Thus with his swollen waist he seemed to fall away both ends. Three times he outgrew his coat. Each time he had eaten till it stretched to bursting point. Each time the process of disrobing was the same.

He dragged his slow bulk to some thick mass of leaves, selected the innermost of them, and spun a web of silk upon its surface. From this he hung himself head downwards. His weight helped him, and, in due course, the old skin split along his back, and he emerged resplendent in a fresh, untarnished, elastic livery.

Each moult was marked by some embellishment. Rusty olive gave place to pale sap green, this in turn to the green of the young willow-leaf, and this again to the green of lush grass. Nor was the change in body colour all. His sides in time were decked with slanting stripes of yellow. A V-shaped orange girdle marked his waist. Its buckle was a tiny splotch of crimson. His horns were tipped with russet brown, and head and tail alike were faintly tinged with blue.

Yet, for all his rainbow tints, Nature had decreed that he should live invisible. To this end she had coloured him to match his food plant. The lines of yellow on his sides broke the monotony of green, as veins break the monotony of a leaf. The blue about him was sister to the blue of summer that played amid the foliage with quivering transparent lights and shadows.

Nor did the cunning harmony end here. In form as well as tint he cheated observation. His outline, as he lay at rest, formed the most perfect outline of a twisted leaf.

Birds passed him by unnoticed. Once, and once only, the ichneumon marked him down.

It was after his fifth and final moult. He was just a shade too light for nature, and the ichneumon has a pretty sense of colour. She buzzed viciously through the foliage, and settled for a moment on his back. She had reckoned without her host. His skin was indeed dangerously bright, but it was sensitive in proportion.

Before she could establish herself, a vicious back-sweep of his horns dislodged her.

Again and again she returned to the attack. Could she but pierce the skin, her paralyzing venom would quickly do its work. Then the murderous task would be easy. Eggs would be laid deep in the wound; grubs would hatch from them, and batten luxuriously on their unwilling host, sapping his strength, but cunningly avoiding his vitals, until they were full-fed. As they turned to pup?he would die, and from caterpillar, or may be chrysalis, there would then issue, in place of gorgeous butterfly, a host of dingy hymenoptera. So would the race of ichneumons be preserved.

The little Emperor was fat and well-liking--an ideal for young ichneumons; but the little Emperor was very wide-awake.

The fly could find no foothold on him. He flung his armed head backwards to his tail. He pawed the air with six fore feet. He shook himself in paroxysms of fury. The fly cared little for the latter, but the horns were hard and formidable. They covered his whole body with their sweep, and struck with lightning speed.

At sundown she withdrew discomfited; the little Emperor's horns had served him well.

His life was uneventful after this. When he had reached a length of two inches, his growth ceased. He fed less ravenously and less frequently. Three parts of his time he spent in contemplation of a special leaf. It was hard to tell wherein lay the fascination. He had spun a silken carpet on it. At rare intervals he tore himself away and snatched a hurried meal, but he infallibly returned to its friendly shelter. He rested on its mid-rib, facing the foot-stalk. His body was strongly arched and so compressed that the ridges of its crowded segments recalled the pile of velvet. His head and fore feet scarcely touched the surface. So he made ready for the second change.

For this even the favourite leaf was discarded. He roamed about the tree for days, seeking one that would suit his purpose. At last he found one, hidden in a thick-set cluster. It hung free, but he secured it in such fashion to its stem that a stiff breeze could hardly shake it. He stretched silken ropes from its edges and passed them completely round the foot-stalk. Then, on its under surface, he spun a little boss of silk, gripped it with his hind-claspers, and swung with easy confidence head downwards. For three days he hung thus motionless, yet within him there was a lively motion.

From the time he left the egg his life had been a dual one. The eye saw nothing but the outward mask, the caterpillar-form. Within this living vehicle that moved and spun and fed, lived the true butterfly--life within life, being within being.

The caterpillar mask had done its work, and having done its work, must die. Yet one can hardly call such dissolution death. As it hung suspended, all the marvellous mechanism which had formed a moving, eating, spinning, sentient being, was absorbed into the chrysalis it covered. Merely the outer empty shell remained.

On the fourth day this shell split cleanly at the tail, and, from the opening, the hind part of the chrysalis emerged. It jerked from side to side, to all appearance aimlessly. Yet there was method in its madness. A side-swing forced it deep into the boss of silk, and, in a moment, the hooks that studded its extremity were fast entangled. The chrysalis had its point d'appui.

Again the old skin cracked, this time behind the neck. The chrysalis head was free. On it were two short, flattened, pointed horns. A jerky movement of the shoulders followed--first expansion, then contraction. At each expansion the old skin slipped a trifle upwards. Turn by turn the segments of the body did their work, until it lay in gathered folds about the tail, just as the pushed-off stocking lies about the ankle.

But even so, the task was not completed. The skin must be got rid of. Its dull white mass, with dangling skeleton horns, was too conspicuous. Nature had armed the chrysalis with the needful tools, a grip attachment and a set of tiny sharp-edged hooks. The skin was fast entangled in the boss of silk. The chrysalis secured an independent foothold (using as stepping-stone the skin itself), spun itself from side to side, and cut the threads that bound it. It jerked lightly from leaf to leaf, until it reached the ground. The second change was accomplished.

Outwardly the chrysalis was nothing but an extra leaf. Colour and form combined their skilful mimicry. Its colour was the green of the sallow; its form, the form of the sallow-leaf.

For fifteen days it hung unchanged and motionless. On the sixteenth change was obviously impending. The upper segments had lengthened, the lower segments had darkened. On the twentieth day came the last great change of all.

It was a normal July day. Thunder was over the Downs. Now and again great rain-drops struck the sallow. They were few and far between, however. The thunder was content to grumble on the hills, leaving the valley to the sunshine. For all the midday heat the air was laden with moisture. This was at once both good and bad for the little Emperor, good because it made the bursting of his cerement easy, bad because it made the drying of his wings slow.

Still he had no choice in the matter; his time had come, and he must make the best of it.

Barely a minute passed between the first yielding of the shell and his complete emergence. He issued head foremost, groping with bewildered legs for something to cling to. He struck the only thing within his reach, the chrysalis case itself. To this he clung with desperation, and he had need to. As yet he had no means of flight.

There is no room for wing expanse inside a chrysalis. Material for wings was lying ready on his shoulders, it was moisture laden, packed in crumpled folds, and lifeless.

* * * * *

The thunder passed away seawards, drawing the valley moisture in its train. From eastward came a gentle drying breeze. It crept from leaf to leaf with its soft-whispered message until it reached the leaf that most had need of it.

The little Emperor trembled with excitement. His wings were coming into being. One by one, like petals of an opening flower, the clinging folds relaxed and told their secret. One by one the branching nervures hardened.

By sundown the great change of all was over. The Emperor, no longer little, was fit to mount his throne. Westward, as if in sympathy, the sky was flooded with imperial purple.

* * * * *

He chose the loftiest branch of the loftiest oak in the forest. Before him stretched an acre of clearing, thronged with his subjects. Every class was represented, or rather every class but one. Ages ago the Swallow tail disputed sovereignty with the Purple Emperor. Fortune declared against him, and he retreated, like some Hereward, to the fens. There to this day he holds a third-rate court.

It was a brilliant gathering that greeted the Emperor. Every colour, every form was there. Whites and brimstones, silver-studded fritillaries, peacocks, red admirals, and painted ladies, walls and ringlets, hairstreaks, blues, and skippers, even the little Duke of Burgundy, even the white and admirable Sibylla.

Happy midsummer children! They flashed their dainty tints from leaf to leaf, from flower to flower, their life one long-drawn revel in the sunshine.

From his high throne the Emperor watched and envied. He was tiring of lonely grandeur. Now and again he soared a hundred feet into the air, then with his wings full spread and motionless, sailed slowly back on to the summit of the oak.

Never was flight more exquisite. As he rose, one caught the glint of the imperial purple; as he descended, its full glory was revealed. Nowhere in nature is the pure radiant effulgence of that purple surpassed. It is the purple of the rainbow itself.

Once, and once only, did he deign to touch the ground. Deep in the hollow behind the clearing, where the footpaths crossed each other, a shallow muddied pool had formed. In it the Emperor saw, from on high, his own reflection. Perhaps it was mere vanity that drew him closer; perhaps the fancy that he saw a rival; perhaps, but this is not likely, thirst. Close to the margin lay a rough-edged clumsy flint. On this he settled, and, Narcissus like, feasted his eyes on his own beauty. He nearly met Narcissus' fate. It was the flint that saved him. He felt the shadow, almost before it reached him, but even so he rose too late. For half a minute he, the Purple Emperor, was prisoner in a boy's straw hat. Had the hat covered the flint completely, he must assuredly have graced a cabinet. Fortunately for him the flint was just an inch too wide. The hat lay slant-wise across it, leaving a narrow crescent outlet on each side.

An old collector would have doffed his coat to cover hat and flint alike, would have sat beside them patiently till nightfall, would have done anything to make certain of his prize. But this collector was only a boy. With youthful recklessness he raised the brim a hair's-breadth off the flint, and, in a moment, the Emperor was fifty feet above him.

It had been a near thing. Higher he soared, and higher, exulting in his freedom, and, as he soared, he sighted the Princess. She sat on an oak pinnacle outlined against the sky. Who was she? Whence had she come? On her wings was the broad white ribbon of butterfly royalty.

The Emperor alighted within a foot of her. For the first time in his life he felt humble. As he opened his wings to show their beauty, she turned her back on him; as he closed them again, she sought another tree. But the Emperor was not so easily baffled. He followed in hot haste, and once more settled on a neighbouring leaf. The Princess drooped her upper wings, as if she was asleep. But she was not. The Emperor crept along the leaves a little closer.

It was the strangest courtship imaginable, for it was all on one side. From tree to tree they went, the Emperor flashing his purple in the sunshine, the Princess, to all appearance, unconscious of her suitor's presence. Yet he tried every allurement he could think of. He circled round her, changing from purple to violet, from violet to velvet black. He soared above her skywards until he was a mere speck in the blue. He showed her the broad ribbon that he also wore. He even uncurled his slender saffron proboscis, and toasted his divinity in the sap of the oak-leaf.

What made her change her mind at the eleventh tree? What had he said to her? I cannot tell you, but I can tell you this. From that tree they rose together, circling round each other. Higher they went and higher, until the oakwood shrunk to a copse beneath them; higher and higher, until the sea was their horizon; higher and higher, until they passed from sight.

THE HARVEST MOUSE

Once upon a time, and not so very long ago either, the Harvest Mouse was the smallest of British beasties, absolutely the very smallest. Even the museum men, who look through microscopes, had to admit that.

Then a Liliputian shrewmouse turned up. He was found stretched dead in the middle of the path, and the time, as any book that deals with shrewmice would tell you, was the autumn. He was so small that, had he not died in the path, he would assuredly not have been found at all.

Now, because of his smallness, and because he was found dead in the autumn (from which you may assume that he was full-grown), he was sent to the museum men; and the museum men examined his teeth, and rubbed their hands with glee, for they found that his upper incisors were abnormal.

So they had his poor little body stuffed, and propped him up with wire in the way they thought he looked nicest, and wrote a brand new ticket for him--SOREX MINUTUS. The lesser shrew. The smallest British quadruped.

Thus was one unique distinction stolen from the harvest mouse. But to this day the harvest mouse shrugs his furry shoulders and says, that there are plenty of dwarfs with abnormal teeth in his own family, if the museum men want them.

He can afford to be superior, for he has yet another unique distinction left, and that is not likely to be taken from him.

Of all the four-footed creatures in Great Britain and Ireland, he, and he only, has a prehensile tail. The middle of it he can bend through half a circle, the last half-inch he can wrap completely round a cornstalk. It is pale chestnut above, and pasty white below. Taken all round, it is the most marvellous tail in the United Kingdom.

A mass of whipcord muscle, it can be made rigid, or flexible, at will. He can sit back with his hind feet resting on one stalk, hitch his tail round another, and lean his full weight against it. His full weight is one-sixth of an ounce. Were the G.P.O. more friendly to naturalists, a score of him could travel for a penny; but, even so, his tail is trivial in proportion.

He is so proud of it that he cleans it continually. Other mice clean their tails at odd times--only when they really seem to need it. The harvest mouse cleans his tail as a matter of regular toilet routine, and he does his toilet fifteen times a day. First his whiskers, then his head and ears, then his body, and finally his tail. He pulls it forward between his hind legs and combs it with his teeth. It is quite worth it.

* * * * *

The harvest mouse sat on the top of a cornstalk and nibbled his supper. His first summer had been most successful. So much had been crowded into it that he could only dimly remember the oat-stack in which he was born. Even the hedgerow seemed difficult to recall. He had lived in that two months, next door to the wood-mouse, and from him he may have learnt something of the art of nest-building. Then he had wandered abroad. The field, on the left of the hedgerow as you walk westward, was, when he entered it, tinged with uncertain green,--a sand-stained green like that of shallow sea. Yet there was cover enough for him. In a week's time, the sprouting corn had got the mastery, shrouding with its exquisite mantle the humble mother soil it seemed ashamed of; then, as if it had imprisoned the sunbeams, it turned to golden yellow, and now, wearying of conquest, had borrowed the copper radiance of a dying day.

It was with the first budding and ripening of the young corn that the harvest mouse tasted the true joy of living. In the hedgerow it had been mere existence; for there had been no real scope for his tail. The grasping portion of it could only encircle the tiniest twigs. Here, Nature herself seemed to have been at pains to suit him. Whichever way he looked, there stretched before him long yellow avenues of pygmy trees. Had they been passed through a gauge, they could not have better suited his proportions. He could whip his tail round any one of them. As he travelled from ear to ear, there was always something handy to grip on to. To reach the top of a cornstalk from the ground took him just two seconds and a half. He ran up it, he did not condescend to climb. Once among the ears, he travelled with little jumps, sometimes waiting for the wind to sway the corn, and help him, sometimes boldly leaping from the summit, and trusting confidently to his tiny hands and feet to pull him up a foot or so below. Even if he blundered to earth he had nothing to fear, for, of all the denizens of the cornfield, he alone could thread the avenues in perfect silence.

The stoat heralded his coming by a stealthy swish that could be heard full twenty yards away. Many a foolish bewildered vole he caught, but never a harvest mouse.

The rat's approach was a blundering four-footed crescendo, clear to mouse-ears as is the ringing of a horse's hoofs to man. Little else appeared at all. Now and again came a foolish hen-faced pheasant, strayed from its nursery, and screaming for its keeper. One was shot as it crossed the path in front of him, but we must not say anything about that. Now and again a corn-crake, moving in silence, bowed to the ground, but betrayed by its loquacity. Now and again a trembling glass-eyed rabbit. To each and every footstep he had one invariable response. He ran up the nearest cornstalk, as high as he could go, and watched the author of it pass beneath him. He was rarely sighted. Once a weasel leapt at him. The weasel is a pretty jumper, but this time a tendril of convolvulus upset his aim. Before he reached the ground again the mouse was five and twenty feet away, playing with his tail.

Half the summer passed before he tired of these diversions. The coming of the sparrows put an end to them. They came just as the corn-ears had commenced to harden. There must have been a thousand. They were not in the field all day, but, while they were there, life was not worth living. Picture it to yourself. A thousand unkempt, shrieking hooligans, plucking at the corn-ears, flinging the milky grain aside half eaten, filling the air with the whirring of their wings as they sighted man a hundred yards away, back again as man departed, quarrelling incessantly, blatant, noisy, vulgar. The cornstalks were no place for mice while sparrows were about.

But the evil had been of short duration. A month had seen the end of it. During that month the ways of the mouse were humble. He wandered in and out the undergrowth, feeding on what the sparrows had discarded. Not that he was really afraid of them. Had they cared to eat him, they assuredly would have done so at the start. But they never missed the opportunity of making him jump, and involuntary jumping is always unpleasant.

However, the life below had its compensations. He would certainly have lost her in the waving maze above. As it was, he saw her at the end of a straight avenue, and he could more or less mark her direction. She was running at full speed, as dainty a little harvest mouse as ever crossed a cornfield.

Her coat was of the softest fawn-chestnut; sharply contrasted with her pure white front, and twisted in a dainty curve to match her features. Her feet and tiny claws were the pink of a sea-shell. Her eyes were small (harvest mice have small eyes), but they were very gentle. As she sighted him, she swung lightly up a thistle stem, and sat for a moment balanced on the head. Evidently he was not altogether uninteresting.

* * * * *

Far into the evening he pressed his suit. When the inevitable rival mouse appeared, half the sun's disk was already masked by the hedgerow. Ungainly, straggling shadows spread across the field, dark bars across a lurid crimson ground. Never was finer mise-en-scene for such a conflict. They fought on the very summits of the stalks, and the sun just managed to see the finish.

* * * * *

They built the nest together. It was his part to bite the long ribbon leaves from their sockets, hers to soften them and knot them and plait them until they formed a neat, compact, and self-coherent sphere.

Nine cornstalks formed the scaffolding. Six inches from the ground she built between them a fragile grass-blade platform. Then she started on the nest itself. Her only tools were her fore-paws, tail, and teeth. The latter she employed to soften stiff material. The weaving she did from below upwards by pure dexterity of hand and tail. For six hours she worked indefatigably, and in six hours it was finished. But it was not meant to live in; it was merely a nursery. All day long the happy pair enjoyed each other's company aloft, leaping from corn-ear to thistle-head, from thistle-head to poppy, and back again to corn-ear, feasting, frivolling, stalking bluebottles. Their life was one long revel in the sunshine; for the harvest mouse has this distinction also, that, like a Christian, he loves the blue of the sky and sleeps at night.

But he is wise in his generation, and lives far from the haunts of men. You must be quieter than a mouse if you want to see him.

At night they lived in a tiny burrow, a foot below the surface of the ground. They had no claim to it, but they had found it empty. Empty burrows belong to the first mouse that comes along.

Once only did they stay above the surface after sundown. For an hour they enjoyed the novel sensation. Then the long-drawn wail of the brown owl drove them below in haste.

Perhaps they realized that prey on the surface is the owl's ideal. It is also the hawk's. But, where under-keepers are armed with guns, the night-bird has the better prospects. Both would have their wings clear as they strike. The owl's great chance comes when the corn is "stitched" in shocks of ten. Then he quarters the stubble, and nothing clear of shelter escapes him.

So the summer had passed--the perfect summer that comes once in a century. Day after day the sun had blazed through a cloudless sky; night after night the dews had fallen and refreshed the earth. The young mice, though pink, as yet, about the nose and waistcoat, were as promising as young mice could be. Everything was altogether and completely satisfactory.

So, as the western sky crimsoned and the shadow of each cornstalk gleamed like copper on its neighbour, the harvest mouse stole down from his eminence and sought his burrow, for, as I have said before, the nest was only a nursery.

* * * * *

He was up betimes. He was a light sleeper, and half a noise of that kind would have roused him. It was clank and whirr and swish and rattle in one. At first it sounded from the far corner on the right; then it passed along the hedgerow, growing more and more menacing until it seemed to be within a yard of him. Then it shrank away to nothing on the left, ceased for a moment, and, in obedience to human shouting, commenced afresh. So from corner to corner, crescendo and diminuendo. The harvest mouse was in the very centre of a square field.

When the sound seemed at its greatest distance, he climbed between two towering stalks and strained his eyes in its direction. He could not see for more than twenty yards before him. The world beyond was wrapt in soft white mist. Never had he seen anything so uncanny. Yet, had he been an early riser, he might have seen it often. Even as he watched it, it seemed to shrink away before the sunshine. The hedgerow loomed like a mountain-ridge before him. Down he slid, making a bee-line for the nest. That was all right; but his wife was evidently perturbed. Her mouth was full of grass-blades, and she was sealing every crevice on its surface. In five minutes he was up aloft once more. The whirring still continued, and now, through the lifting haze, he could distinguish its origin. Horses it was for certain, ay, and men--a small man sat upon the leading horse; but there was something behind these.

Had the harvest mouse ever seen a windmill, he would assuredly have concluded that a young one had escaped, and was walking in ever-narrowing circuits, round the field. The mist lifted further, and he saw the thing more clearly. Its great red arms swung dark against the sky, gathering the corn in a giant's grasp to feed its ravenous cutters. Round and round the field it went. Each time as it travelled to the distant corners the mouse dropped down to earth; each time as it thundered close at hand, he dashed like lightning up the stalk to look. Sometimes his wife came with him. Closer it drew and closer. Nor was the mouse the only thing that noticed it. All things that lived within the field, all things that loved its borders, were crowding in mad confusion to its centre.

First came the hare. His was a wild, blundering, panic-stricken stampede. He hurtled through the corn, crossing his fore feet at every second leap, his eyes starting backwards from his head, his ears pressed flat against his back. He passed the harvest mouse heading for the farther side, and the harvest mouse saw him no more, for he broke cover, trusting to his speed. Then, one by one, bewildered rabbits. Backwards and forwards they rushed. Now they sat up and listened; now they flung their white tails skywards, and vanished down some friendly seeming alley. In two minutes they were headed off.

Among the rabbits, of all things, a stoat! The mouse crept two grains higher when he saw him. He stole in and out the undergrowth with easy confidence, yet in some sense unstoatlike. The mouse looked down, and for a moment caught his eye--the most courageous eye in all the world. Something was very wrong indeed with the stoat--he never even bared his teeth.

Next, a flurried brood of nestling partridges, flattened to earth, and piping dismally to one another. Time after time they passed and repassed below him, until at last they were utterly weary, and crouched in a huddled mass together, with uplifted hunted eyes.

Then the rats and mice and voles. House-mice and wood-mice, red voles, and grey. Last of all, Berus the adder. Not a mouse stepped aside, as he worked his slow, sinuous length between the cornstalks. He, too, was of the hunted to-day.

Nearer and nearer drew the hoarse rattle of the reaper. More and more crowded were the few yards round the harvest mice. A large brown rat limped through, bleeding about the head. He had come in from the firing-line, and had incompletely dodged a stone. The stoat flung its head up as it scented him, but let him pass. He had never let a rat pass in his life before.

* * * * *

Only a square of forty yards remained, packed from end to end with desperate field-folk. Each prepared for its last stand in different fashion.

The rat selected a stout thistle-clump, planted his back against it, and sat back on his haunches. Berus the adder made a flattened spiral of his coils, and raised his head a trifle off the ground, ready to fling his whole weight forward from the tail. The pheasant chicks ceased piping, and lay still as death. The red voles and wood-mice dashed aimlessly to and fro. The stump-tailed voles trusted to the ludicrous cover of the broken ground. The stoat arched his back and bared his teeth to the gums. But the harvest mice sat on the top of the stalk and awaited events, to all seeming unmoved. Perhaps they were too small to be frightened. They were certainly too small to be confident. Yet, as things turned out, the top of the stalk was the safest place of all. Swish went the cutter. The nest was scattered to fragments before their eyes, and the rush began.

The rabbits started it. They flattened their ears, shut their eyes, and made a blind dash for the open. Not a rabbit escaped, for there were dogs. The rats fared no better; they held their ground to the last, and were mercilessly bludgeoned. The partridges were cut to pieces. Most of the mice and voles shared their fate. The stoat died game. He charged one yokel and routed him. Then he was set upon by three with sticks. In the open the stoat is no match for three with sticks.

Berus the adder lay still in a hollow. The cutter passed completely over him. He was always ready, but his earth-colour saved him the necessity of striking. As the evening shadows lengthened, he stole grimly from his shelter, crossed the field, climbed the slope, and regained his furze-bush.

And the harvest mice? The mother-mouse dashed to her nest as she saw it falling, and a wheel of the reaper passed over her. The father-mouse was saved, but through no merit of his own. Until the reaper was actually upon him, he clung to his stalk with tail and eighteen toes. Then it was too late to leave go. The great red arms gathered his stalk in the midst of a hundred others, swept the whole on to the knives, and dropped them on the travelling canvas platform. Up he went, and down again. For a moment he thought that he was stifled. His eyes started from their sockets. His ribs seemed to crumple within him--fortunately they were elastic, as ribs no thicker than a stout hair must be. Then the pressure relaxed. The automatic binding was complete, and one more sheaf fell with a thud to earth. In that sheaf was the harvest mouse, bruised but alive, a prisoner in the dark. The stalks pressed tight against his body; but for the pitchfork he could never have got out.

The pitchfork shot through the middle of the mass, and missed him by half an inch. Once more he felt his surroundings flying upwards, but this time they fell more lightly. They formed the outside of a stitch of ten. As the fork was withdrawn the binding of the sheaf was loosened. He could breathe with comfort, and he could also see. He peered out, and found the whole face of Nature changed. The waving cornfield had gone. In its place was a razed expanse of stubble. The corn-sheaves stretched in serried piles across it. The harvesting had been neatly timed. Behind the hedge was the crimson glow of sunset. After all, that had not changed.

For an hour he waited within the sheaf, dubious and uncertain. Then he stole from his shelter. Within five yards he found her, gripping the shattered fragments of the nest. Close by lay a bludgeoned rat, and, five yards farther on, there sat a living one. It had its back to him, but by its movements he could see that it was feeding.

The field was flooded with moonlight. On all sides resounded the ominous hum of beetles' wings. Nature had summoned her burying squad. They had their work cut out, and blundered down from every quarter. For death had been very busy, and it was not the death that needs seeking out. About the centre of the field the ground was stained with smears of half-dried blood. So the beetles came in their thousands, and before morning broke their task was done.

But the harvest mouse did not wait till the morning. The fragments of his nest were empty, and he dared not look to see what the rat was eating.

He reached the sheaf-pile only just in time, for the brown owl was still abroad, quartering the field with deadly certainty of purpose. As he crept beneath it, he heard the brown rat scream.

His was the last sheaf to be piled, it was also the last sheaf to be lifted. It travelled to the stack on the summit of the last load, and, by a happy chance, formed one of the outside layer. By scratching and gnawing continuously for an hour, he worked his way to the butt of it, paused for a moment on the precipitous steep, and then scrambled lightly down to earth. A perpendicular descent was nothing to him.

The foundations of the stack were already tenanted. Some of the inmates had been, like himself, conveyed in sheaves, but more had rushed for shelter across the bared expanse, which, on all previous nights, had been a cornfield. There were mice of all kinds, there were half a dozen rats. Before a week had passed, like had joined like. The rats were undisputed masters of the basement; midway lived the common, vulgar mice; and, highest of all, as befitted them, for they only could thread the interstices of the upper sheaves, and they only had prehensile tails, the harvest mice.

THE TRIVIAL FORTUNES OF MOLGE

It was a bubble that launched him into a practical existence. They were rising by hundreds from the ooze that cloaked the bottom of the ditch. The sunshine called them up and scattered them into nothingness as they appeared. It was merely by chance that one, in its upward rush, hit his envelope of starwort; it was merely by chance that the envelope needed no greater stimulus to burst asunder.

Yet he was arranged to take advantage of the smallest jar. Like any other newt, he had started life as a small white rounded egg; for ten days he had remained, to all outward appearance, the same; cunningly enfolded, neatly glued down, but still an egg. Then the temperature rose, and he changed from sphere to cylinder, from cylinder to clumsy crescent, from crescent to watchspring. The core of the watchspring was his head, the extremity his tail, and, when the bubble touched him, he flicked out like the works of a Waterbury. His first colour sensation was the green of thick glass. As he sank, it grew dimmer and dirtier and browner, and presently, as he reached the ooze, it was blotted out.

He was straight, but unlovely--nothing but two black lines and three dots, cased in a filament of jelly. The lines were destined for his backbone and stomach; the dots for his eyes and mouth. The latter was ready for immediate work, given only the impulse. As he sank slowly, head downwards, the impulse was supplied. Out from his neck there floated two sprays of gossamer network, of such delicate texture, such dainty tracery, that nothing but the gentle laving of water could have unravelled them and left them whole. Through them the water flowed, and with it came the dim consciousness of individual life, the dim instinct of self-preservation. As he touched the bottom, the middle dot resolved itself into a sucker.

Fortunately his tastes were vegetarian and indiscriminate. For three days he contentedly sucked in his slush surroundings, and, in that time, the two outer dots bedecked themselves with rings of burnished copper. He could breathe, he could eat, he could see.

On the fourth day he could move. The black lines had also played their part. Both had intensified, but not equally. The uppermost had outstripped its fellow. For half its length it now ran alone, tapering to its end and carrying with it a ribbon envelope, transparent and invisible as glass.

Its use he learnt by grim experience. When first he moved it, it drove him headlong into inky darkness. His gills crumpled in the rough embrace of the mud, and his eyes and sucker were choked with slime. It was only a desperate, convulsive, aimless wriggle that freed him. The next time he cleared his immediate surroundings, and shot a full six inches upwards, only to sink slowly to the ooze again, motionless, and exhausted. He had described an elegant parabola.

Day by day his excursions grew longer and higher. Nor were they without adventure. Sometimes he would be caught in the wake of a stickleback, and would reach the bottom spinning, or on his back. He was lucky to reach it at all. Sometimes a sunbeam's dazzling radiance would check him in mid-career, and his callow eyes would take an hour to recover. It was a month before his eyelids developed. Sometimes he would collide with others of his own kind, equally unskilled in steering, and sometimes a vague quiver in the water caused him instinctively to mimic death, and thus avoid death in reality.

In a week's time he had grown out of all knowledge. To be accurate, he had doubled in size. But, even then, it was only the copper gleam of his eyes that saved him from utter insignificance. The remainder of him, for the most part of jelly transparency, was invisible against his sombre surroundings. His sucker had taken the semblance of a mouth, his gills were longer and more feathery, the curves of his tail were more shapely, but still he was, as yet, the merest apology for a tadpole, and so he remained until his limbs grew. They came in front at first--froggy's come behind, he wants them to swim with--the most curious spindle-shanks of arms that can be imagined, with elbows always flexed, and fingers always stretched apart. In due course his legs followed, of like purpose and absurdity. For swimming he only used his tail, but for balancing and steering, his feet and hands. Would he rise to the surface, he must flick his tail, and turn his toes and fingers upwards. Would he seek the bottom, he must depress them. Would he lie motionless, suspended in mid-water, he must point them straight outwards from his sides.

It was the charm of a free-swimming existence that divorced him from a vegetarian diet. To be continually sucking in plant sludge was a low grubby business at the best. Besides, he was now furnished with a respectable pair of jaws, not to mention the rudiments of teeth. Daphne was his first victim. Daphne sounds somehow floral, but this Daphne was equipped with one eye and several pairs of legs, and practised abrupt jumpy flights through the water. In short, she was a branchiopod, to be vulgarly precise, a water-flea. The succulence of Daphne led to experiments on Cyclops--Cyclops is her first cousin--and the taste, once acquired, never left him.

It was in the pursuit of this latter that he lost a leg, and thus realized that the problems of existence before him were twofold: he must not only eat, he must avoid being eaten. It was probably a stickleback that took his leg. A more powerful enemy would have taken the whole of him. So intent was he on his quarry that he scarcely realized the severance until he found himself swimming in an aimless lopsided circle. Then he sought the friendly shelter of the weeds, and sat still to ruminate. The leg was undoubtedly gone--his right hind leg--it was nipped off close to his body. He felt no pain, but, the moment he left his support, he realized that he was at a great disadvantage. The more studied his efforts to progress straight, the more certainly abnormal was his course. In letting himself sink slowly to the bottom he showed prudence. It was only at the bottom that he was likely to escape notice.

He stayed there for a succession of days, getting hungrier and hungrier, for it was only the smallest fry that came within his reach. It was lucky for him that his gills lasted out. It was a full month before a new leg commenced to fill the vacancy, and, by that time, they had shrunk from feathery exuberance to two ugly stunted tufts. It was the most painful period in his whole career. Every day his breathing grew more laboured. Instinct told him to seek the surface, but, each time he made the effort, he capsized before half the distance was accomplished. In six weeks' time came relief. He had not yet secured a new leg, but the growing stump fulfilled its purpose. He reached, by strenuous efforts, the surface of the water, opened his mouth and breathed the air.

But for his unfortunate accident, it is probable that the transformation from a water-breathing to an air-breathing animal would have accomplished itself imperceptibly. It is likely indeed, that, for a short period, while his gills were decrepit, and his lungs infantile, he might have breathed air and water alternately and at will. Now, however, his gills were, for all practical purposes, useless; his lungs, ready but unpractised. The necessity of air-breathing was forced on him at a moment's notice.

Small wonder that he commenced by overdoing matters. To begin with he distended himself so that he could not sink at all. Then he sank with far too small a reserve, and struggled to the surface spluttering and half-drowned. It was only after much tribulation that he adjusted matters to a nicety, diving with just sufficient air-supply to last his purpose, and emerging at the proper moment. A silver bubble, the waste product of his life, marked his downgoings and uprisings.

What made him quit the water altogether? For days he had lain half-submerged on a mass of starwort, his limbs idly anchored off his body, his quaint, puckered face and goggle eyes fixed immovably on infinity. He was, to all appearance, carved in stone when the impulse took him; and then--it was as if the swimming instinct had left him--he commenced to crawl across the natural bridge of pond-weed to the bank. Nor can I tell you where he went. Sometimes you may meet his kind in dark, damp corners, wedged between stones, or in the crannies of fallen tree trunks. Sometimes it is the gardener that brings word of him. "A' dug the spade a fut deep and turned he up, the poisonous effet, a' soon stamped on he!" Sometimes it is the housemaid. "Please m'm there's lizards in the cellar, I dursn't go near." Sometimes a halfpenny head-line. "Can Life be Indefinitely Prolonged? Startling Discovery in a Lump of Coal." But, wherever he may have got to, I can assure you of this, that for three whole years he stayed there and never willingly saw the light of day. Nature looked after him in his seclusion, Nature brought him such food as he required, and Nature never forgot him, but guided him back in due course to the brook in which he first saw light.

* * * * *

He was a dingy object from above. His eyes, it is true, had kept their tadpole lustre, but his coat had darkened to a dusky olive, and the only vivid colour about him, his orange waistcoat, was invisible as he crawled.

Even if it had been visible it would not have been to his disadvantage. Of all the colours in Nature there are none more warning than contrasted black and orange. Show me a creature of this colour combination, and you will show me something that is dangerous or nauseous or poisonous. It was this, perhaps, that was his salvation as he crawled from his land retreat back to the water he had left three years before. Perhaps it was simply his insignificance, for the journey was made by night, and he was crawling in and out of thickly twisted grass stems. Perhaps, though, it was his appearance, which, I will freely admit, was at this time, repulsive. A low set ridge along the centre of his back, and a faint violet tinge upon his sides were all that told of the glory that was to be.

He glided into the water slowly, and, as it were, ashamed. But he need not have been. In three years' seclusion he had swelled to fair proportions. He was no longer of necessity the hunted, in most cases now he was to be the hunter. As his head parted the surface, myriads of frightened atoms fled panic-stricken before him. Each lash of his tail scattered a microscopic community, and, as he progressed, the sense of mastery grew upon him. Food was here, and in plenty. He had only to open his mouth and take his fill. Yet he had no appetite. For the first few days of his water existence he sat amid the weed, rising only at rare intervals to the surface for air, and eating nothing. He was feeling the sudden change. His skin was tense and drawn all over, so tense, indeed, that each time he opened his mouth he felt the strain of it. Nor was the discomfort in his mouth alone. His coat was stretched to bursting-point along his back; his limbs seemed cased in gloves a size too small. A crawl ashore brought no immediate relief, but helped him indirectly. As he brushed between two grass stems, the skin of his lips split asunder, and, when he entered the water again, that friendly element gently forced its way into the gap. Every forward movement that he made now eased his old worn skin a little backwards.

First his head came free, and its old covering lay in tattered rags upon his neck. He pulled his hands out next, leaving their casing as the fingers of a turned glove. Next came his body's turn, for this he had to squeeze himself between the weed-stalks. Lastly, he cleared his legs and tail.

His old skin hung before him on the starwort, white-gleaming and transparent, a perfect, neatly folded model of himself. Of himself, did I say? It scarcely did his present splendour justice. Along his back now rose the budding undulations of a crest. His flanks had lost their sombre olive shade, and were suffused with mottlings of velvet black, mottlings that turned to purple as they crept across his orange front.

Even these beauties paled before his tail--a ribbon whose jet black centre shaded into violet, and whose edges were flushed with crimson.

Had he not been consumed with hunger, he might well have lingered in complacent admiration of himself. But hunger such as he had never felt before rose superior to his 鎧 thetic sense, and he left his weed-shelter in ravenous haste.

He had not far to go--a swim of ten yards, and he was among the tadpoles.

They were in a patch of sunlight, lazily browsing on the starwort, mild as any sheep, with foolish, staring eyes, gaping suckers, and bodies that gleamed as if sprinkled with gold dust. For three days he settled in their neighbourhood, growing each day sleeker and more gorgeous. His orange waistcoat took a warmer hue, the crimson deepened on his tail and tipped the summits of his festooned crest. In six days' time he was a very perfect newt, decked and caparisoned for love or war. The very sticklebacks fought shy of him. One, it is true, charged him with spines erect--he had a nest to guard and would have charged a pike--but even he, for all his burnished panoply of emerald and vermilion, shrank back and bristled defiance from a safe distance. As for the shoal, they scattered in flashing rainbow-tinted disarray at his approach.

He was master of his surroundings, but there came a time when tadpoles palled upon him. For one thing, they were becoming daily more bony. Those with hind legs developed were difficult to swallow; those with front legs also were hopeless. A change of diet was imperative, and, in seeking for this, he came into collision with the water-spider.

Now, the water-spider lived by himself in a bubble of his own making. His legs were stout and long and hairy, his countenance was horrible, and his bite a thing to be avoided. When the newt first saw him he was devouring a caddis-worm. Vanity had been the worm's undoing. Instead of casing itself with tiny sticks and pebbles and sojourning at the bottom, as Nature ordained, it had put on a gaudy livery of starwort leaves. Trusting to this elegant protective mimicry, it boldly sought the surface. The disguise availed it nothing. The spider drove its fangs through the flimsy covering that but half concealed its head. The newt had seen it all. The bunch of animated foliage carelessly advancing, the spider's leap from its bubble, the glint of its shears as they met in the wretched creature's neck, the ghastly quivering tremor of the case. Then the fierce eight-legged efforts to extract the victim, and finally the awful cunning that seemed intelligent of Nature's devices, and pulled it out, as any angler would, tail foremost.

It was not so much animus against the spider as a longing for the worm that brought about the conflict. For the newt to snap at it was certainly unpardonable. Had he anticipated the resultant display of force, he would have hesitated. He had judged the spider solely by his size. When he felt six legs firmly fixed about his face, when he felt the cunning leverage of two more added to the pull, and a hideous pair of jaws drawing closer and closer, he dropped the worm, a useless martyr in Nature's scheme, and bit for freedom. The spider lost a foot, but left its mark, and the spider's hairy foot was not worth eating.

In his next robbery he was more judicious. He snatched an infant dragon-fly from the jaws of the water-scorpion, devoured it with pleasure, and then turned his attention to the water-scorpion himself. He found him flat and tasteless. The water-boatman was more succulent, but, with only one soft spot, difficult to do justice to. It was the same with all the larger creatures. He was reduced to stickleback fry, small larvae, and even juveniles of his own race. But nothing touched the tadpole, whose unkind destiny it is to furnish half the water-world with food. Had it not been for a diversion, he would have left the water in disgust.

* * * * *

Probably it was a case of mutual attraction. He swung his tail and crest before her, comeliest and most debonair of all her suitors; and she, with an engaging smile, swung a responsive tail at him. Crest she had none, and, of course, her tail could not compare with his in beauty. The higher we get in the natural orders, the more distinctly does decoration become a feminine necessity. Her coat was a pale olive green; her front light orange. Her charm was in herself.

For newts they made an excellent and well-matched pair. Of course they had their disagreements. Newts are by nature fickle and inconstant.

When she was occupied with the cares of a family, and spent her days and nights in deftly fashioning starwort cradles for her eggs, it was irritating that he, whose duty it was to frighten the marauding sticklebacks, should have preferred to rush away into the giddy vortex of newt society. It was more than irritating when, by way of showing that her cradles were insecure, he opened six and devoured the contents himself.

She profited by the experience, however, and the next series were exquisitely finished. The egg was placed in the exact centre of the leaf, the leaf was folded over, and sealed, tip to base, with all the strength of her hind feet. Her mouth put the finishing touch.

When she had visited some half-dozen stalks, and left each adorned throughout its length with a neat series of symmetrical bows, she felt that her task was done and that she was at liberty to accompany him. Together they learnt the brook from end to end. Sometimes they walked along the bottom, stirring to right and left of them a host of low-class life, slimy leeches, dingy crustaceans of every imaginable kind. Sometimes they traversed the middle deeps, brushing against the beetles and the boatmen and the water-snails. Sometimes they sunned themselves on the surface, snapping idly at the measurers and whirligigs.

It was the flood that parted them. For three days it had rained unceasingly on the surface of the brook. As they rose to breathe, their noses were lashed by pigmy waves. Each raindrop made its own widening eddy, its own pattering sound. Rain on the roof is noisy enough to those beneath, but rain on the water is deafening.

In the brook, as I have said, it rained for three days. In one part or another of the valley it rained for a week. The meadow-land gave its surplus to the brook, and the brook sought the river for relief. But the river was already filled to overflowing, so that brook and river met each other halfway, and the life in each was intermingled.

Now, between brook-life and river-life there is a great gulf fixed. There is no sideways in the river. All things that would stay at rest obey the current. The fishes point their noses against it; the plants lie as it guides them. Up or down is the law of quiet existence. The newt knew nothing of this, and, when a rush of waters swept him into the river-bed his natural instinct was to seek the bank. This laid him broadside and helpless. A roach snapped idly at him as he floundered past the shoal. The snap cost him his tail, and was probably his salvation. Without a tail his biteable area was halved. A young trout missed him, and he pulled up amid the lamperns in the shallows. The lamperns were too busily engrossed to notice him. Each was fast anchored by its sucker to a rounded pebble. Across their slender undulating bodies he struggled to the shore, battered, bruised, and tailless, but alive. He entered the first brook he came to, and there he remained a month in gloomy solitude, for he felt that his chief glory had been taken from him. In a month's time his tail had partially repaired itself. The new portion was stubby and colourless. In another fortnight his crest had shrunk to half its former size. This blow decided him. He left the water definitely. Where he went I cannot tell you, nor do I know what happened to her, but I think they will meet next year, and by that time his tail will be as beautiful as ever.

THE PASSING OF THE BLACK RAT

(NOTE.--The old English black rat, for some three hundred years predominant in this country, is now well-nigh extinct. He has been superseded, some think exterminated, by the brown Hanoverian rat, a more powerful and disreputable species, which made its appearance in the course of the eighteenth century.)

The black rat sat back on his haunches, pricked up his ears, and listened. It was something different to the faint lapping wash of the sewer; different to the dull hum of the traffic. It was an uncanny, unfamiliar scratching.

Every rat knows the scratching of his relations; but the black rat had no relations.

Six weeks ago there had been at least two others of his kind in existence--the one he had fought with, and the one he had most unsuccessfully fought for. As a matter of fact, he had crawled away from that encounter to die. Instead of dying, he had recovered. That his rival was in reality the better rat he could not allow. Position is everything in the rat duello, and position had not favoured him.

After a series of disastrous frontal attacks, he had limped behind the old corn-bin, with half his mouth torn away, and his front paws mangled and useless. He had bowed his head and waited sullenly for the coup de grace. But the coup de grace never came. There had been a diversion in the rear, and into the cause of that diversion he had not troubled to inquire.

He had seen neither him nor her since, and, until he had recovered from his wounds, had hardly felt his loneliness. For a wounded rat, loneliness is normal and necessary. Of late, as he sniffed dubiously round the old familiar corners, the sense of desolation had forced itself upon him.

He recalled, dimly, the few weeks before his misfortune. Every day the number of the tribe had lessened. First went the patriarch, white about the muzzle, grizzled all over, tottering and feeble, but still of eminent distinction--the black rat does not coarsen with age--then, one by one, with fearless inconsequence, the younger ones; lastly, save two, his own contemporaries.

* * * * *

The scratching seemed to get louder. The black rat glided, like a shadow, towards it. It sounded from the bottom of the door.

Three sides of the cellar--for a hundred years the cellar had been the rats' stronghold--were solid masonry. The fourth side was a wooden partition. At one corner of this stood the door, close-fitted to its sill and frame, and shrouded in cobwebs, which, in rats' memory, had never parted. Along the wall opposite ran a six-inch shelf, and, at the extremity of this shelf, where the fittings entered the brickwork, was the entrance of the run.

Generations of rats had used that run. Its sides were smooth and polished as a metal tube. Here it was narrower, there wider, but throughout its length it was free and unimpeded.

For the most part it lay between wall and wainscot. At times it seemed to pierce the masonry itself. Midway in the ascent the path of least resistance had been towards the outer wall. Two round holes pierced its surface--a brick's length dividing them. One can understand the making of the first hole, but the making of the second? Fifteen feet below resounded the busy traffic of the city. Did two tunnels converge by chance? did they converge by design? or was the second made by some colossal rat, stretched at full length, and trusting his life to his superhuman hearing? I can only state the facts. I do not pretend to explain them.

From the second hole the run passed into the masonry once more, zigzagged upwards into the storeroom, and ended.

From the storeroom there were countless exists--down the gutter into the courtyard (a short cut to the shambles), beneath the flooring to the scullery, and thence along the drain-pipe to the great sewer, through the ventilator on to the roof--anywhere, everywhere.

* * * * *

The scratching was certainly louder. The black rat was stepping very delicately, but a slippery corn-husk shot from underneath his foot, and with the rustle of the corn-husk the scratching ceased.

Nothing but a rat could have heard that; it was certainly a rat, but who?

For ten minutes he waited, listening. Then he stole forward, until the points of his whiskers brushed lightly against the door. Instantly there was a movement on the far side--a four-footed movement. Caution against such cunning seemed superfluous. He boldly forced his nose between door and flooring and sniffed; but only for a second, for his nose had gone farther than he meant; the bottom of the woodwork had been gnawed through until it was a bare half-inch thick all along its length. He drew back with a jerk, and waited another ten minutes, staring at the door and thinking.

The silence on the far side grew unendurable. The black rat whisked round, and rushed madly for the run. He gained the shelf by a beautiful swinging leap, easy and silent as a cat's.

For the first few yards, between brickwork and wainscot, the run was clear enough; but, as it turned upwards to the floor above, something seemed unfamiliar.

The light, which had always faintly shimmered from the hole in the outer wall, was gone. As he drove forward headlong, he bruised his nose against the cause of its disappearance. The wall had been repaired with concrete. It was utterly ungnawable, and he slowly retraced his steps to the cellar. He was just in time to hear the scratching recommence.

It drew closer and closer. It got upon his nerves. He tried to steady himself by nibbling at a stray corn-ear. He dropped it before he had fairly tasted it, and crept forward to the door once more. There was more than one unknown at work. At times a light quiver ran the whole length of the bottom ledge.

From a rat standpoint, it was the worst position conceivable. That attack was impending was certain; it was equally certain that retreat was impossible. Desperation, rather than bravado, determined him to reverse the positions. In one spot the wood had been fined to a quarter of an inch. Light filtered through, and cast a dull red shadow on the floor. It was at that spot that he flung himself. As he touched it, every other sound ceased. He had the field to himself, and he worked it to the best of his ability. The splinters flew before his chisel teeth; he wrenched, and scratched, and tore. Before five minutes were gone, the flimsy wooden screen had been transformed into a neat three-cornered hole.

He thrust his head forward, and stared with all his eyes. At first he could distinguish nothing. The far side of the partition was, in comparison with his recent surroundings, brilliantly lighted. Gradually the form of the enemy shaped itself before him. It was certainly a rat, but what a rat! Until his muzzle had shot through the opening, it had been facing him, waiting and watching. Now it had leapt backwards, and presented a three-quarter rear view.

It was the most vulgar, ill-conditioned beast he had ever set eyes on. Its muzzle was coarse and blunted; its ears were half concealed in coarse-grained, unkempt hair; its tail, instead of tapering, like his own, to an elegant infinity, was short and stumpy; its eyes were, to say the least of it, insignificant. But its colour! a dirty, nondescript, khaki brown!

The sight of it was enough, and he drove at it full tilt.

Appearances were undoubtedly against the brown rat, but it knew something of tactics. With a lightness, such as one could hardly have expected, it swung to one side, and, before his brilliant charge could take effect, had got its back to the wall. He had made the same mistake again--the mistake of brainless breeding all the world over. It mattered not whether he approached from front, or right, or left, the same whirling flail of fore-paws was ready for him. He leapt clean over its head, and was flung back--by the brickwork. Whichever way he tried he had only half a foe to aim at. Still he never flinched, happy in the conviction that blood must tell.

Blood might have told against a single enemy. Against a score it availed little. And a full score were advancing. The ungainly, stubby forms seemed to rise from every crevice in the floor.

They came very slowly at first--a dirty cohort of khaki Hanoverians; their muzzles uplifted and quivering at the scent of blood, their beady eyes fixed seemingly on vacancy, but really on himself. He felt them coming, and, for a moment, paused in his attack. The whole group might, save for the restless nostrils, have been carved in stone; the duellists eyeing each other warily, the scavenger ring waiting on events; but the whiskers of each one trembled, and gave the whole group life.

It was the watchman's tread that broke the spell. The black rat knew that tread well enough. He knew every tread in the warehouse; but to the invaders it was unfamiliar. Before the footsteps had resounded twice, he was left alone; the host had vanished as quickly as it came.

The black rat retreated in good order, and established himself once more in a corner of the cellar. It was a mistake, but he wanted time to recover himself, and time to think.

Of the world on the far side of the partition he knew nothing, but he realized that there was a world. Should he make a rush for it before the enemy had regained courage? Even so, where should he rush to? Was he likely to find an exit amid altogether strange surroundings? Could he block the hole? Rats had done such things before now, but it was only deferring the evil hour, and what time would he have to do it in? The question was answered for him. The echo of the watchman's step had barely ceased, before the hole at the base of the door was, for a moment, obscured.

They came in jerky disorder. First a young, loose-limbed stripling. He was barely out before he was back again, throwing up the pink soles of his hind feet, and flicking the woodwork with his belated tail. Then a kaleidoscopic succession of suspicious faces. The light danced on the floor as each thrust his neighbour aside, thrust his head like lightning through the opening, and as quickly withdrew it. They were masters of scouting, these brown barbarians. Sometimes one, bolder or younger than the rest, would steal a foot within the cellar. Sometimes, for minutes together, all would be quiet, the light patch on the floor the only thing amiss. The black rat never moved his eyes from that light.

It was an hour before the chieftain himself appeared. He squeezed through the opening, but, for all his bulk, came quickly. Once clear, he dropped upon his haunches, and knit his fists before him. The position showed him at his best. Crouched or in motion, the clumsy angles of his body were forced into relief. As he sat back, the curves softened, and, as far as brown rat could be, he was imposing. For some moments he sat immovable, facing the darkness, then he turned, and, with one eye always fixed behind him, passed slowly out of sight.

There was a long silence after this. The light patch on the floor seemed to grow in intensity. By its dull reflection, the black rat could just distinguish his own whiskers. It fascinated him. He stole halfway across the floor towards it, and paused. As he paused, it was blotted out once more.

He was being watched. Before he was back in his corner, three of the enemy were through the breach. Five more followed. Then in quick confusion a dozen. Then a dozen more. The Hanoverian army was spreading its wings.

Their actual number he never knew. Perhaps, for the credit of his family, it was as well. Reflection would assuredly have put resistance, and even hope, out of the question. As it was, he came forward with absolute indifference. His breeding again stood him in good stead. Of all the host he was the least uneasy. In the middle of the floor he stopped abruptly, confronting the situation. Fifty rats were in the cellar now, and there was not a rustle among them.

He had calculated exactly where to stop. It was a foot beyond the normal take-off of the grown rat. He flung his head round, put all the force he possessed into his hind legs, and leapt, upwards and backwards, towards the shelf. He caught it with his fore-paws, scrambled on to it, and, for the moment, was safe. He was only just quick enough. As his eyes turned, the brown rats had rushed forward, and, even as he clutched the ledge, he heard them pattering against the wall.

The floor below was a raging sea of rats; rats leaping over one another, jostling, biting, tearing. To the silence of a moment before had succeeded a babel of shrieks and hisses. But there were no jumpers among them like himself. He passed quietly along the ledge above them, through the entrance of the run, and up to its blocked extremity. There he braced his back against the concrete and waited.

* * * * *

He waited for three days, his muzzle grounded, his eyes peering into the darkness, his every sense alert. He ate nothing, he drank nothing--to all appearance he never slept.

On the fourth day, he crept feebly halfway towards the cellar. Privation was beginning to tell on him. His only hope was that the invaders might have retired.

For the first few yards it almost seemed as if it was so. Neither in the air nor on the ground could he detect the slightest vibration; but, as he turned a sharp corner, the hope was dispelled. The whole run quivered with the stealthy whisper of rats' footsteps. Faint squeaks and whimperings echoed along it. The cellar was evidently still occupied in force; he was cornered between starvation and insuperable odds. Yet there might be a scrap of food this side of the cellar. He stole forward until another turn revealed the ledge. In the centre of the ledge were three brown rats. The farther one was cleaning itself, but the other two were feeding, and, at the sight of the food, he lost all prudence. He was upon them before he was perceived. The two dropped their provender, leapt blindly forward, and fell clumsily to the floor below, but the third slid down the junction of the walls.

The black rat realized what that meant. As he turned his head, he saw his retreat cut off. Two more had scaled the corner behind him. He swung about to face them, girded himself to charge, and, instead of charging, stopped dead.

For the first time in his life he knew what fear was. Before him were his immediate adversaries; his quick ears caught the crumbling of plaster behind him. Rats were mounting that corner also.

Five feet below lay the floor. Its surface glistened with shifting beads of light--light from rats' eyes.

He was between the devil and the deep sea--the floor was the sea, and the devil was assuredly advancing towards him. Never before had he set eyes on such a beast--ten inches from head to tail, brawny, misshapen, mangy, a veritable Caliban of rats.

The position was hopeless. All he could do was to die game. Caliban had crept within a foot of him, and was pulling himself into position. But he was too slow. Before he had raised his clumsy fore-paws from the ground, the black rat's teeth had met in his throat. His huge frame quivered for a moment, staggered, and lurched heavily off the shelf. He carried his comrade with him.

First blood! what matter whose? Caliban lay where he fell, his eyes slowly glazing. The eyes round him caught the reflection from his throat. He was the hero of a hundred fights, and the puniest ratling had its share. The floor was for the moment the centre of attraction.

Had it not been for the chieftain, the black rat might have regained the run. But the chieftain had foreseen events. As Caliban fell he had clambered up, and was now blocking the entrance.

He was grounded on his haunches, with uplifted paws, ready for anything. The black rat drove at him, and was hurled backwards. Among rats the chieftain is, of necessity, pluperfect master of defence. Again and again he parried the attack, until Caliban was disposed of.

Then, in the middle of his rush, the black rat heard once more the stealthy footstep in his rear, paused, half turned, missed his footing, and fell.

Yet he accounted for four of those below, which made five altogether.

"THE FOX'S TRICKS ARE MANY; ONE IS ENOUGH FOR THE URCHIN" (Old Greek Proverb).

Rain, and rain, and rain. For three days in succession the sun had defaulted. Yet he had been doing his best behind the storm-clouds. That very morning he had forced one straggling beam well through. It had been completely thrown away, for every living thing was snugly tucked up under cover. Now, as his time was getting short, he made one last despairing effort.

Westward, the sky was banked with purple nimbus, towering in gloomy magnificence aloft, but fined to nothingness on the horizon. The sun saw his chance, and took it. As the storm-cloud was borne a trifle upwards, he flashed his dying radiance beneath it.

At first the brightness was intolerable. The rain-drenched leaves were bathed in liquid fire; the river surface gleamed like molten metal; the undergrowth that fringed the bank became a tangled web of dazzling light-points.

The effort was of short duration, yet, before the sun had sunk, the things that loved the river had caught his message.

The cloud-bank lifted sullenly, and dispersed. Out of the east came a soft summer breeze, stealing silently across the valley, and tilting the balance of each dripping leaf. So the great drops of moisture slipped off them to swell the river, and the drying of the earth commenced.

That is what brought them all out together.

The water-rat came from a hole five feet above the river-level. An overhanging grass-tuft masked her exit. As a rule, she used the back way--a gently sloping tunnel which led from nest to stream. But to-night it was very still. She padded quietly to the water's edge, slid through the reeds that bordered it, and sat upon a silted crescent of mud that lay on their far side. She always sat there to commence with. From the bank she was invisible; up stream and down she could see for fifty yards, and the pith of the reed-stem, of all things in her menu most charming, lay ready to her orange-tinted teeth.

The noctules came from the hollow in the old chestnut. Twenty of them lived there together, because it was a convenient, roomy hollow. No one knows how it started--perhaps the wood-peckers could tell you--but rain had certainly finished its excavation. The entrance was some thirty feet above the ground--dank, noisome, and forbidding; the end was near the roots.

Of course the old chestnut was dying; but that did not concern the noctules. Each evening they crawled up to prove the weather; each evening, of late, they had shambled back again into the gloomy depths, cannoning awkwardly against each other, snarling and grumbling. The temper of bats is uncertain, and hunger does not improve it.

But to-night it was better. One by one the ghoulish muzzles emerged, peered into the darkness, and were satisfied; then the clumsy, ill-balanced bodies, entangled in loose-folded leathern cerements--the noctule's wing-spread measures a full foot; lastly, the webbed curving triangle of feet and tail.

Each, as it blundered free, clung, for a space, head downwards to the bark, then slacked the grip of its ten toes, unhooked its thumbs, dropped, and flew. Never was flight more graceful, never more perfectly controlled. For fear of the swallows, the summer beetles fly by choice at twilight; even then they must needs fly low, for the noctule never misses, and the crunch of his teeth in a beetle's horny back is all he knows of music.

The stoat came from a tree which was even more decrepit than the chestnut. It had been an elm once. For four centuries it had defied the elements, towering full fifty feet in rugged, imperial grandeur. The elements had outstayed it. All that remained was a caverned stump, whose jagged summit pointed, like an accusing finger, to the sky.

But, from a stoat standpoint, the stump was unsurpassable. There were three exits from the hollow base. Up the shaft there was yet another. Thick brambles fringed it on every side, and in those brambles were many birds' nests. The stump was an ideal nursery; as such the stoat had employed it. He had left to its friendly protection his family of six, with a young rabbit to keep them occupied. He, himself, was now in quest of frogs.

The hedgehog bore on his back clear tokens of his last retreat. A dozen withered leaves were clinging to his spines. The nearest pile of such lay heaped against the hen-house. The hedgehog footed through the knotgrass slowly, grubbing with his snout to right and left of him. Sometimes, when cover failed, he broke into a bow-legged run.

The squirrel came from high up in the beech tree--the second fork from the top. There he had built what he called a nest, but what humans, with greater nicety of diction, call a drey. Speak not of squirrel's "nest" to sportsmen; to speak of fox's "burrow" were hardly less heinous. The drey was eminently satisfactory, for, in the summer months, it was completely hidden. Yet three days inside it had been more than sufficient for the squirrel. He was cold, hungry, and cramped in every limb. To quicken the blood within him, he flung himself at lightning speed from bough to bough, from tree to tree, up and down the branches, in and out the maze of dripping foliage, until his every hair was tipped with a raindrop, and he was almost weary. Then he paused a moment for breath and shook himself, dog-fashion.

The mole's uneasy, crimson-pointed muzzle came from a hole right on the water's edge. He was feeling for the water. Last night the swollen river had forced its way a yard into his run, and he had blundered headlong into it. Swimming is easy to the mole, but swimming in an inch-wide tube is risky. So, to-night, he was cautious. It might have been fine all day, or it might have been wet, for all he knew.

The grass-snake seemed to come up from the river bottom. His head suddenly parted the water beneath the old pollard, and he swam slowly across the stream, craning his neck before him. The pollard was inwardly rotten to the core--a snug retreat for snakes, to which the only entrance was a water-way.

The dormouse came from halfway up the hazel, and the wood-mouse came from its roots. They, too, had been three days weather bound; but they were not hungry. Each had its winter store to draw upon.

The moths and caterpillars and beetles, came from everywhere--crannies in the brickwork, joints in the palings, crevices in the bark, from neat-rolled envelope of leaf, from hollowed shelter of reed-stem, from pigmy burrows in the ground.

* * * * *

It was the hedgehog who started it. The hedgehog has a keen sense of humour, and, for that reason, he loves an argument.

"I will back my spines," said he, "against any means of defence in the country." He curled himself into a forbidding spiky ball, and rolled slowly down the bank towards the water. On the very brink he stopped and uncurled himself. "Or any means of offence," he added.

This was too much.

"Spines!" sneered the stoat. "Spines might be some use if you had any pace behind them. Where would they come in against a hare?"

"Spines would be awkward in the shallows," murmured the water-rat, as she swam quietly over to the far shore, keeping half an eye on the stoat, who was also something of a swimmer.

"Spines!" squeaked the noctule from the safe height of a hundred feet. "Why load yourself with spines? Why not fly like me?"

"Spines!" shouted the squirrel. "A pretty mess you'd make of it with spines up here. Do you think every one spends their life grubbing after ground beetles?"

"Spines!" purred the moths. "We gave up spines at quite an early stage. Haven't you finished moulting, hedgehog?"

"Spines!" snapped the trout. "Give me a good set of fins."

Now this was exactly what the hedgehog had foreseen. As I have said before, he had a keen sense of humour.

"I am willing to hear you all," said he.

So, because of his pleistocene lineage, and because of his popularity (the comedian is always the more popular candidate), and because he had started the discussion, he was voted to the chair.

The noctule spoke first. He leant his arm against the roughened bark, hooked his thumb-nail into a crevice, and opened his mouth as though he would eat the world. He was not beautiful, and his voice was three octaves above F in alt. What reached the audience below was somewhat on these lines--

"I and my kin are the only mammals that fly. Therefore I am superior to the hedgehog. Flying is the best state of all. Even the humans do their poor best to fly. Every part of me is modified for flight. My knees bend the wrong way so as to better stretch my wing-membranes. My tail serves as a rudder, and in the hollow pouch about it I can trap a beetle, ay, and carry him where I will. My sense of touch is the most delicate in all the world. I never dash myself, like blundering bird, against a wire. If you would know the secret, look at the trembling bristles on my muzzle, look at the earlets within my ears, look at the sensitive wing-membrane between my fingers. No quiver in the air escapes me. I have the sixth sense of the blind, and yet I see."

Next spoke the stoat, the swash-buckler. He cleared his throat with a short, rasping bark, glared round him, and began--

"I am the only flesh-eater among you all," said he. The hedgehog's smile broadened, but he said nothing. "Therefore I have bigger game to tackle than any of you. Therefore I am better armed. Scores of bats I have eaten in my time. I could climb your chestnut if I cared to, noctule, and eat the colony. I would, if you were not so evil-smelling." (This from the stoat!) "Scores of water-rats have I eaten, too. Look at my long, lithe body. What burrow is too small for it? Look at my teeth. What rodent has a chance against them? I fear nothing, not even man himself. I can swim, I can run, I can climb, I can hunt by scent, and I am cunning as a fox. From my fur, when I am dead, comes the imperial ermine. Would you pit yourself against me, hedgehog?"

"I would," said the squirrel. Like the bats, he was some way off the ground; also he had mapped up a clear course of forty yards among the tree-tops, so he spoke recklessly. "The stoat is an amateur climber." ("Wait till I get to your nursery!" snarled the stoat.) "He has no idea of taking cover. A treed stoat against a human is doomed. Look at his black-smudged tail--only a trifle better than a weasel's. It reminds me of my summer moult--but it's worse; and, in the summer, even I must trust more to my hands and feet. I, the most skilful gymnast in the country, save only the marten, and there are too few of them to count. Give me my winter parachute, and see me then. Who can thread the woods like me? From end to end I fly, skimming the tree-tops and never touching ground. Yet, if the fancy takes me, I can cover land or water faster than any stoat. From my fur, when I am dead, comes the camel-hair brush."

Next came the dormouse. "Sleep is the best defence of all," he said. "Sleep and being very small indeed, and never coming out except after sundown, and having great big eyes, so that you can see things like stoats long before they see you. Offence I know nothing of, unless it's eating beetles."

After him the wood-mouse. "Give me a good burrow underground," said he. "Make it among branching roots, with half a dozen entrances and exits, and I defy the weasel, let alone the stoat. But in the winter, when cover is scanty, sleep and a store of nuts is best of all. Beans are no good--they rot away. Earth-stored nuts, tight packed, are the sweetest things I know."

"What of summer?" said the hedgehog.

"Weight for weight," said the mouse, "I can tackle anything that moves. As for voles and house-mice, I can fight two at once. When I am giving much away, I like my burrow handy."

"Who talks of burrows?" said the mole. "Where is there tunnel-builder like myself? Two fields away you can see my fortresses. You can see them plainly, tunnelled maze and rounded nest and all. Some prying human has turned his vacant mind to nature-study, and made a clumsy section of a pair. Look at each in turn. Mark the one tunnel that leads upward to the nest, mark the two galleries that surround it, mark that they wind in a spiral, and are not joined by shafts at intervals. That would so weaken the surroundings as to leave the nest an easy prey to scratching weasel. Why is the spiral made? To cheat inquiry; a dozen tunnels join it from the run; from it are a dozen exits to the surrounding field. One tunnel only leads into the nest. Only the moles know that one. Alone I did it, save for my wife, who hindered me. Alone I moved two hundredweight of earth. Nor do my qualities end here. Were I fifty times as big, I would be lord of creation. Where can you find fiercer courage than mine; where, bulk for bulk, more mighty strength? What monster, think you, would an elephant, built for burrowing, be? For my weight, I am the strongest thing that lives. One creature, and one only, approaches me; that is the mole-cricket. Let him speak for himself."

The mole-cricket turned up from nowhere in particular, and his voice was the tinkling of a silver bell. It would have taken a score of him to make a mole.

"I am older than the mole," he said, "yet from him I take my name. In dry ground I make poor progress; where it is muddy and swampy, I can run through it, like a fish through water. When the mole came into being, he borrowed the pattern of my fore feet--shovel and pick and spade in one. Like me, he learnt to run backwards or forwards, and that is why his hair has no set in it. Whichever way he goes, the clinging dust is swept from off its surface. He comes from grubby depths as polished as a pin. And so do I; but from a different cause. I am so highly polished that the damp soil cannot cleave to me."

"Burrowing," said the hedgehog, "is a low form of defence. What says the water-rat?"

"I burrow, too," said the water-rat. "If I have time, I burrow in the water. I part the surface with the tiniest ripple, keeping my fore feet close packed to my sides, and swim with hind legs only, below the surface, neatly as a natterjack. If I were better treated, I should never burrow in the banks at all. But I must have somewhere to go to when my breath fails me. I eat the mare's tail and the pith of reed-stems. That does no one any harm, not even a trout-preserver. But of all good viands, commend me to a parsnip."

"This is neither defence nor offence," said the hedgehog.

"The only offensive thing I have is a pair of incisors," said the water-rat. "They are orange-yellow and very strong. As regards defence, I can do more in the water than most."

"Not more than me," the young trout broke in. He flung his nose jauntily against the surface, and the surface swung from it in widening eddies, circle after circle. "I can be up to the weir and down again before you are halfway across the stream. When humans build their destroyers, they model them on me. I know that, because I have seen their clumsy models, trout-shaped, save the mark!"

"That is enough from any one of your years," said the hedgehog. "Little river-fishes run away from big river-fishes, and big river-fishes run away from bigger river-fishes, and they all run away from the otter."

The jack that lived in the deep below the pollard grinned, but said nothing. The jack knew better, but he never says anything. But the gudgeon and the troutling were terrified at the notion of bigger fishes, and made straight for the weeds.

"What think the caterpillars?" said the hedgehog.

The caterpillars were studying moral invisibility in a hundred different ways, for insect life is the most highly specialized of all. It was the lobster-moth-to-be that spoke first. He bent his head backwards until it touched his tail, folded the knee-joints of his skinny legs, and began--

"It is all bluff," said he, "caterpillars are past-masters of bluff. Look at the hawkmoths, fat, flabby, bloated things, with curly tails. Most of them fling their heads back, arch their necks, and play at being snakes. Some grow eyes upon them, not real eyes, but markings which serve as such, enough to scare the average chuckle-headed bird. Sometimes they trust to vein-markings on their bodies, which turn them into casual misshapen leaves. Sometimes they liken themselves to twigs--"

"That is what we do," cried the loopers. Each branch of the oak had its loopers, feeding cheerfully, transforming themselves to twigs, and shamming death in quick succession.

"Sometimes," continued the lobster-moth-to-be, "they are, like myself, really worth eating. Then, mere vulgar imitation bluff is of little avail. To be a withered leaf is my first line of defence; if the ichneumon buzzes nearer, I shift my ground and become a spider. I am the only caterpillar in the country with spider-legs; when they are stretched to their full length and quivering, they are worse to look at than the real thing. Should even this fail me, I show the imitation scar on my fourth body-ring. That usually clinches the matter. The ichneumon fondly imagines that I am already occupied. So, if I am lucky, I turn at length to dingy pupa, and thus preserve my race."

"Will you hear an amphibian?" said the toad. He came from the centre of a grass-tuft, and spoke with solemn deliberation. "Not one of you is more persecuted than I. From time immemorial I have been the loadstone of credulity, and--I am altogether defenceless. I am never worth eating, for the shock of capture opens every pore on my skin, drenching me with what the poets class as venom. So I am usually thrown aside with a broken back. For centuries I was thought to have a jewel in my head. How many of my hapless ancestors were tortured for that jewel! With the toad's death, the jewel was believed to vanish. How many have been 'larned to be a toad' by baffled, disappointed rustics! That is what puts the sad expression in my eye. How have I survived it all? By dogged perseverance. I lay so many eggs that one at least must survive. Thus is the balance of the race preserved. I myself was one of five hundred, the only one that reached maturity. Yet all were in the same long ribbon coil. The swan that gulped the coil, gulped all but me. I dropped into the brook alone, and there I quietly passed through my novitiate, egg to tadpole, tadpole to toadling, toadling to toad. When my tail was absorbed into my body, I sought a land-retreat. There I have spent my time for twenty years. None of you know it, and none ever will. I leave it only at twilight, and, as you pass, I shield my face with my fore feet. Froggin is much the same; nothing but his prolific quality saves him."

"Froggin is at least worth eating," said the grass-snake. He lay with all his four-foot length displayed in graceful sinuous curves, and was listened to in silence. Nothing loves a snake, however harmless. "With me, as with the caterpillars, it is mostly bluff. I can swing back my head, and flatten the nape of my neck, as well as any deadly adder. I can also strike, but there is no poison behind the blow. My only weapon of offence is smell, a sickening musty smell, that makes the enemy loose his hold. Once I am halfway down a hole, I'm safe. I set my ratchet scales against the sides, and nothing can dislodge me. Only a jerk is dangerous, and that must be accomplished before I am fairly fixed."

"I am armour-clad," said the stag-beetle. "Could there be better method of defence? Look at the sliding joints of my breastplate. Human skill has copied it, but never has surpassed it. My horns look formidable, but for offence are useless. They are far from my eyes, and move but slowly. Give me time, and I can crush a tender twig between them, and suck its juices. That is all the purpose they serve me, yet they look like branching antlers, and that also is something."

"I have heard you all," said the hedgehog. "I have heard the flier's point of view from the bat, the gymnast's point of view from the squirrel, the swimmer's point of view from the water-rat, and the assassin's point of view from the stoat." For a moment he coiled himself up with a snap, but the stoat made no remark, so he slowly uncoiled himself, and resumed. "Yet I maintain my original contention, there is nothing like spines. 'The fox's tricks are many; one is enough for the urchin.' What is the one unfailing, all-sufficing trick? The proper and judicious use of spines. All of you would use spines if you could. Most of you do. Think of the bramble-thickets, think of the furze, the last resort of valiant stoat and viper, think of the holly, where the sparrows roost.

"Spines are the proved asylum of the spineless. Nature has flung them broadcast. She starts low down among the plants, thorn and thistle, gorse and cactus. Then she turns to the sea-urchins and caterpillars and beetles, then she fashions the globe-fish and thorny devil-lizard, then she comes to the birds--spikes are their only weapons--lastly, in me and mine, she reaches the fulness of perfection.

"Think of the purposes spines serve me. Which of you defies the fox or terrier in the open? I leave the fliers out--running away is not defence. To me a fight is child's play. The more inquisitive my foe, the tighter do I clinch myself together. They get more harm than I do."

The last few words were spoken from within. The stoat approached gingerly, and turned the hedgehog over, seeking for a place to jump at. The bat wheeled across him, and swerved at the suspicion of those rigid spears. The caterpillars betook themselves once more to feeding. The water-rat slipped quietly down the stream,--she still feared the stoat. The squirrel ran openly down his tree-trunk, and secretly up the far side of it. The fear of the stoat was on him too. So the moon rose, and, for most, the chance of sport that night passed away.

The hedgehog remained coiled for an hour. Then he shambled away, well satisfied. First he eat two pheasant eggs, then a belated frog, and then a nestling blackbird. As the sun mounted the eastern sky he once more sought the pile of leaves that lay against the hen-house.

THE END

www.ingramcontent.com/pod-product-compliance
Lightning Source LLC
Chambersburg PA
CBHW062020280526
45787CB00005B/2173